"Brent Hunter's book, *The Rainbow Bridge*, highlights religious traditions' common theme — the need to cultivate inner values like love and compassion if we are to create a happier, more peaceful world. This commonality is the main reason why we can say that the core essence of all the world's major religions are the same and that they should co-exist harmoniously in the service of humanity. I believe that readers who are interested in love, kindness, inner peace and a better world may find much in this book to inspire them."

— H.H. the 14th Dalai Lama

"From the beginning of time all we've ever wanted is to love and be loved, and from the beginning of time all we've ever done on this planet is make it nearly impossible to experience our highest desire. That is because we have imagined in our illusions that one of us is somehow better than another. This idea of "betterness" has created divisions between religions, between cultures, between people and between nations. The idea is also a false thought, directly contradicting the greatest teaching of all religions in the world which, put into one sentence, reduces itself to a simple truth: We are all one. *The Rainbow Bridge*, a wonderful treasure conceived by Brent Hunter, is a demonstration of that truth that you can hold in your hand. Once held in your hand, you will hold it in your heart as well and it will illumine your soul."

— Neale Donald Walsch, N.Y. Times bestselling author of the five-book series *Conversations With God* (Books 1, 2 and 3), *Friendship with God* and *Communion with God*

"*The Rainbow Bridge* is a must-read book for anyone who wishes to understand the common ground in the world's major wisdom traditions, to understand what binds us all together, and to understand what steps we might take to create a bridge to a better world."

— Dr. Reza Aslan, N.Y. Times bestselling author of *Zealot* and *No god but God*

"I like to say that we can either take control of our lives or someone else will. *The Rainbow Bridge* is a powerful example of how we can take control of our future by coming together, united by a common vision of peace, to create a better world for all. Let's work together to make world peace a reality by creating a new global operating system for the 21st century."

— Dain Blanton, Olympic Gold Medalist, sportscaster and motivational speaker

"The Rainbow Bridge highlights time-honored values – service, kindness, and the sanctity of the life process- in service of a better future we can create together. Readers of all ages will find in Brent Hunter's collection of original aphorisms and powerful quotations inspiring fuel for contemplation as well as an uplifting introduction to some of the greatest mystics, both ancient and modern."

— Andrew Cohen, founder of EnlightenNext, author *Evolutionary Enlightenment*

"Brent Hunter's Rainbow Bridge wonderfully illuminates Einstein's statement: 'When the solution is simple, God is answering.' This simple, profound and practical path, graced with marvelous examples, of how individuals and nations can live in peace is a must read for all. Thank you, Brent, for such a joyful and demonstrable book."

— Bill Froehlich (writer-producer *MacGyver, The Outer Limits*, co-author *U R The Solution*)

"Religions of the world are increasingly becoming more and more divisive. My Grandfather, Mohandas K. Gandhi, once said: Unfortunately mankind has learned just enough from religion to hate and not enough to love. He also said: religion is like climbing a mountain. Everyone is ultimately going to reach the same peak, so why should it matter which side of the mountain one chooses to climb? In his book *"The Rainbow Bridge"*, Brent Hunter exemplifies these Truths. If humanity is to be saved from utter doom it is important that all of us, individually and collectively, take the first step to learn from all the religions of the world that love is more powerful and positive than being consumed by hate. *The Rainbow Bridge* is the first step in the right direction."

— Dr. Arun Gandhi, President, Gandhi Worldwide Education Institute (GandhiForChildren.org)

"Our great wisdom and spiritual traditions across the planet and through the ages converge on astounding findings- they all call us to find the miraculous bridge within to cross from the separation of ego-based life to the higher ground, the higher script, the awakened global mind, where we enter the Unified Field of Sacred Presence. Whether the call of Tao, or Aum, or Yahweh, or Christ, or Allah, or Buddha's Emptiness...they all share the same fundamental diagnosis that ego-based life brings individual and collective human suffering of all kinds, and that finding the sacred bridge -the rainbow bridge- that reveals and models the secret of unity-in-diversity and diversity-in-unity is the crossing to the higher life of peace and joyous living. Brent Hunter's timely book flows from a wealth of personal experience and confirmation over the years and brings into the open the fundamental principles- the global principles- that are embodied in our diverse great teachings through the ages. This book is open and accessible and rings of authenticity. It deserves careful heart reading by those who wish to find the bridge to human flourishing in our global age."

— Dr. Ashok Gangadean, Author of *Awakening Global Mind* and *Awakening Global Enlightenment: Our Maturation as a Species*

"Brent Hunter's *The Rainbow Bridge* overturns the doom and gloom mindset that is so prevalent today. Brent gets down to explore the worm's eye details of the biggest challenges facing our planet while zooming out to the big picture perspective. In addressing terrorism for instance, Brent acknowledges that poverty and lack of hope are root causes of terrorism and to solve our global problems, including terrorism, we must address the root causes. *The Rainbow Bridge* highlights that global problems require global solutions. The book's message of hope brings to life the old adage from the great visionary inventor Buckminster Fuller who acknowledged, 'You never change things by fighting the existing reality. To change something, build a new model that makes the old model obsolete.'"

— Ron Garan, highly decorated fighter pilot, astronaut and aquanaut

"*The Rainbow Bridge* is truly the bridge to world peace starting with inner peace – this is just what humanity needs right now."

— William Gladstone, author of *The Power of Twelve*, *The Twelve* and *The Golden Motorcycle Gang*

"*The Rainbow Bridge* is one of those rare books that you find once in a blue moon. It is an inspiring book that celebrates diversity on a global scale and contains eye-opening ideas that will help create a better world. Let's come together in the name of peace and sanity, and grow into a global movement of peace in our lifetimes. Thank you, Brent Hunter, for your vision and for your profound contribution to peace in the world. I heartily recommend *The Rainbow Bridge* to everyone who desires inner peace as well as world peace."

— Louis Gossett, Jr., Academy Award-Winning Actor, Author, Entrepreneur and Elder Statesman

"*The Rainbow Bridge* is a therapeutic trove of wisdom – truly bridging all our traditions, beliefs and deepest aspirations for our human family and common future!"
— Hazel Henderson, evolutionary economist and author, *Ethical Markets: Growing the Green Economy*

"As an Olympic Pentathlete I had an amazing experience using only mental rehearsal to place second at the Olympic Trials for my third Olympic Team. *The Rainbow Bridge* is a powerful book and a groundbreaking project that can bring large numbers of people to engage these same abilities to envision and take collective action to create the peaceful world we all want to live in. It is an exciting moment in history and *The Rainbow Bridge* is an example of a world-class project that is innovative, inclusive, and engages our highest creative capabilities.

I am inspired as I work with Olympians around the world and with a committee at the United Nations to see how shared purpose ignites a level of creativity and teamwork. *The Rainbow Bridge*, especially the 14-point Road Map to World Peace, is an effective strategy that can bring people together and turn a common vision of world peace into reality. The principles identified in *The Rainbow Bridge* are universal principles that people everywhere can identify with and they are our 'rainbow bridge' to the future."
— Marilyn King, Olympic Pentathlete 1972/1976; Founder, Beyond Sports

"I highly recommend *The Rainbow Bridge* to everyone who cares about living meaningfully and making a difference in our troubled world. It is an inspiring book, focusing on important universal principles. At one level it is a book about our shared experiences of living, dying and dreaming. At another level, it is a book about responsibility for ourselves, each other and the world. *The Rainbow Bridge* is filled with hope and simple wisdom in the tradition of Lao Tzu that one can return to again and again."
— Dr. David Krieger, Founder and President of the Nuclear Age Peace Foundation (www.wagingpeace.org); author of *Hope in a Dark Time, ZERO: The Case for Nuclear Weapons Abolition* and more

"The Rainbow Bridge summarizes the common spiritual heritage of mankind. It is the shared resource we need to enter on a path that bridges our problems and leads us to a world worthy of the highest aspirations of a species that not only has consciousness, but can and must have planetary consciousness."

— Dr. Ervin Laszlo, Founder and President of the Club of Budapest, systems theorist, integral theorist and prolific author

"We all are dreaming of achieving Inner Peace and we all are hoping to witness World Peace in our lifetime. Brent N. Hunter's book *The Rainbow Bridge,* now in its 4th edition, shows us the ways to cross this visionary Bridge, carefully constructed with Love, Compassion and Wisdom. Trust your mind that you can cross this Bridge, open your heart and you will be surprised what you find on the other side of the Rainbow Bridge so enticingly laid out by its author. You will feel enriched and rewarded."

— John W. McDonald, U.S. Ambassador ret., Chairman and CEO Institute for Multi-Track Diplomacy and Christel McDonald

"Seeing the Earth from a great distance, astronauts see a single interconnected world with no physical boundaries where we are all one family of humanity. That vantage point also shows us the absolute need to come together to peacefully solve our issues. Brent Hunter's book *The Rainbow Bridge* is a treasure that can help lead us in the right direction. Let's move forward together to help create a new global operating system that works for all of humanity."

— Dr. Edgar Mitchell, Apollo 14 astronaut and sixth man to walk on the moon, founder of the Institute of Noetic Sciences (IONS), author and lecturer

"Brent Hunter has written a book to be read again and again. Rainbows are visions and Brent shows how we all share common truths and a global vision. As the song says 'someday we'll find it, the Rainbow Connection' and it starts here with *The Rainbow Bridge*. And in time we will achieve the happy world my late husband, Dr. Robert Muller, believed is possible."

— Barbara Muller, Literary Agent and Global PR for *Most of All They Taught Me Happiness* (GoodMorningWorld.org)

"In a world of frills, diversions and dangerous detours we find ourselves lost without true guidance. Once again Brent Hunter brings us the guidance we need from the essence teachings of the wisdom traditions. Just when we think we have met the wall a bridge appears. Take it."

— James O'Dea, International social healer, peacebuilder, teacher, author and former president of The Institute of Noetic Sciences

"*The Rainbow Bridge* is a breath of fresh air during challenging times. It is a bold and groundbreaking book that should be required reading in schools and universities around the world. This book should be talked about around our dinner tables and in the media. Thank you, Brent Hunter, for showing us how we can bridge the gap between war and peace, to a better world for all."

— Governor Bill Richardson, former UN Ambassador, Governor, U.S. Energy Secretary, Congressman and founder of The Richardson Center for Global Engagement

"The world is waking up to what Brent Hunter has been saying for a decade. The new planetary era we are co-creating must be infused with wisdom – wisdom which is the foundation of most spiritual approaches today. You will love the quotes that run throughout the entire book. It occurred to me that this would make a great book to put by your bedside so that you could thumb through and read and reflect on the wisdom of each page. Hunter brings us up to the current era by, including such newly formed movements as the global commons and offers a living path to a meaningful and purposeful life within the challenges of the 21st century."

— Dr. Nancy Roof, Founder/Editor Kosmos Journal

"This profound gem is packed with a deep well of insights and wisdom. Communicating in a heartfelt way, with a clear desire to unify humanity, Brent Hunter gives us a roadmap to the conscious evolution of humanity. A book to carry, consult often and give away to all those you care about."

— Dr. Elisabet Sahtouris, evolution biologist, author of *EarthDance*

"Being a pioneering adventurer and a global citizen, I have raised my universal peace flag at three poles of the world. As an honorary diplomat, I have pursued unconventional methods of diplomacy in the promotion of universal peace. Brent Hunter's groundbreaking book, *The Rainbow Bridge*, is a must-read for anyone who dreams of a better world and wants to know how we can get there. Let's come together to make world peace our reality now."

— Namira Salim, Virgin Galactic Founder Astronaut

"Holding a positive image for humanity is a transformational act. Connecting what we can be as a civilization with who we are as a complex and varied people is the bridge work that will allow us to live into our roles as agents of love and peace. *The Rainbow Bridge* is a much needed operating manual that will help us reach our highest potentials- individually and as a multicultural family. This book is a must read for all who hold the image of our collective greatness."

— Dr. Marilyn Schlitz, Ambassador of Creative Projects and Global Affairs, Institute of Noetic Sciences

"Diversity in religion, spirituality and culture is an unqualified good for humanity. Gandhi said in his time that 'The friendly study of other religions is the sacred duty of each one of us'. Now more than ever we need to become experts of the major traditions of spirituality and religion. To do so will allow our collective understanding to see the common ground we all stand on in our various faiths. Brent Hunter is a person with a mission to spread the acceptance of pluralism around the world. His book, *The Rainbow Bridge*, is a gem reflecting rays of wisdom from all the traditions of the religions, pointing to the common ground among us. We must learn to be comfortable on this bridge because it is our future."

— The late Dr. Brother Wayne Teasdale, author of *The Mystic Heart: Discovering a Universal Spirituality in the World's Religions*

"*The Rainbow Bridge* is a beautiful vision and a practical set of principles and practices to realize what His Holiness the Dalai Lama likes to call for, "World Peace Through Inner Peace!" Great thanks to Brent Hunter! It can be envisioned, enjoyed and crossed over by anyone, whatever their religion or non-religion, if they just trust their own imaginations, and let themselves embrace the positive. I recommend *The Rainbow Bridge* to myself and to all of you, safe and sound always as it gently and blissfully arches through our inmost hearts."

— Dr. Robert Thurman, President of Tibet House US, prolific author and speaker

The Rainbow Bridge

Awards/Recognition For *The Rainbow Bridge*

1. WINNER: Gold Medal, 2015 Reader's Favorite Book Award (Religion/Philosophy)

2. WINNER: 2015 Pinnacle Book Achievement Award (Inspirational)

3. WINNER: 2015 Beverly Hills Book Award (Inspiration)

4. WINNER: 2015 Beverly Hills Book Award (Spirituality)

5. WINNER: 2014 USA Best Book Award (Spirituality: Inspirational)

6. WINNER: 2014 National Indie Excellence Award (Body/Mind/Spirit)

7. WINNER: 2014 Los Angeles Book Festival (Spirituality)

8. WINNER: 2014 B.R.A.G. Medallion

9. WINNER: Gold Medal, 2014 Global Ebook Awards (Gift/Specialty)

10. WINNER: Silver Medal, 2014 Global Ebook Awards (Current Events/Politics/Foreign Affairs)

11. WINNER: Bronze Medal, 2014 Global Ebook Awards (Inspirational/Visionary)

12. WINNER: Notable Indie Book, 2014 Shelf Unbound Writing Contest

13. WINNER: 2013 Bronze Medal for World Peace

14. RUNNER-UP: 2014 San Francisco Book Festival (Spirituality)

15. HONORABLE MENTION: 2015 Paris Book Festival (Spiritual)

16. HONORABLE MENTION: 2014 London Book Festival (Spiritual)

17. HONORABLE MENTION: 2014 New York Book Festival (Spirituality)

18. FINALIST: 2014 Wishing Shelf Book Award

19. FINALIST: 2014 International Book Award (Spirituality: Inspirational)

20. FINALIST: 2014 Next Generation Indie Book Award (Social Change)

21. FINALIST: 2014 Next Generation Indie Book Award (Spirituality)

22. FINALIST: 2014 Next Generation Indie Book Award (New Age)

Also by Brent N. Hunter

The Pieces of Our Puzzle

Nuggets of Wisdom

More Nuggets of Wisdom

The
Rainbow
Bridge

Bridge to Inner Peace and to World Peace

Brent N. Hunter

Spirit Rising Productions
San Francisco, CA • Los Angeles, CA

Spirit Rising Productions

ISBN: 978-0-9912064-4-5
Library of Congress Control Number: 2013920666
Edition: Fourth
Format: Paperback
Published: 2-28-14
Updated: 9-24-15

Spirit Rising Productions
2261 Market Street, Suite 637
San Francisco, CA 94114

Visit our website at SpiritRising.TV

Cover art by Daniel B. Holeman
(web site: AwakenVisions.com)

Printed in the United States of America

Dedication

This book is dedicated to
the children and people of young spirit
to whom the future truly belongs.

"Build a bridge before the river swells."

Thangtong Gyalpo

Table of Contents

Preface

2014 marks the 13-year anniversary of the first edition of *The Rainbow Bridge*. The first edition, published in 2001, was titled *The Rainbow Bridge: Universal Book of Living, Dying and Dreaming*, and illuminates the common ground in the world's wisdom traditions, also known as universal principles. The second edition was published in 2003 and was translated into 23 languages by fans around the world, to whom I remain eternally grateful. In 2011, the third edition was published, *The Rainbow Bridge: Bridge to Inner Peace and to World Peace*. In 2013, the third edition won the Living Now 2013 Bronze Medal for World Peace. This fourth edition represents the most significant upgrade since the first edition was published 13 years ago.

Within the core of all four editions you will find the universal principles. I have been consciously living my life according to these principles and their wisdom has stood the test of time. This ancient wisdom is as profound now as it was 13 years ago, and using universal principles now is more important than ever before.

This fourth edition includes additional concrete practical actions we can take to help shift our collective future in a positive direction as we collectively create a bridge to a more just and peaceful future.

Brent Hunter

January 15, 2014
West Hills, CA

PART ONE

Introduction

*"Believe nothing,
no matter where you have read it or who has said it,
not even if I have said it,
unless it agrees with your own reason
and your own common sense."*

— Author Unknown

Intention and Origin of *The Rainbow Bridge*

The intention of this book is to create a bridge that will help lead humanity from our current world filled with poverty and violence to a wisdom-based global culture of unprecedented love, harmony, cooperation, and unity.

We can indeed create peace and harmony on this planet and we have everything we need — right here, right now. If we take it one step at a time, it's an achievable goal. But *how* are we going to take on this Herculean task?

We must start by understanding the current situation in which we now find ourselves. We must ask the most profound and yet basic questions such as "Who are we?", "Where are we?", and "What is the purpose of our lives?" Great mystics and leaders from all of the world's major wisdom traditions have been teaching the same messages for thousands of years.

Although this book is not about me personally, it is important to share something about myself so that you have a better understanding of where I'm coming from, as well as a greater appreciation for the information presented in this book.

I've been in the world of business and information technology since discovering computers in high school. Since then I've received advanced education and professional certifications in knowledge management, change management and project management, and have held positions from programmer to systems analyst to CIO to CEO to Chairman. As a result, I tend to use logical examples from the world of computers and technology, which you will see throughout this book. I'm also a former psychotherapist and National Certified Counselor.

Perhaps more interesting than my professional background, I've spent most of my life pursuing a spiritual path, engaged in the process of "becoming." Having practiced transcendental, as well as other forms of meditation since age 12, I have been in pursuit of knowledge and wisdom through intense mental, introspective, psychological, physical, and spiritual studies. Being born part Muslim, part Jewish and raised as a Christian, with a father who had a deep interest in meditation and Buddhism, this journey has not always been easy. I discovered that the great perennial wisdom of all of the various religious perspectives was never available in an integrated form.

The information in this book is the fruit of decades of hard work and study. The common ground I am about to unveil comes from my own direct experience — several years of extremely challenging and extraordinary experiences, relative to the earlier times in my life. During this period of challenging, near-mythological ordeals while running a business, I kept notes of what I considered to be of vital importance. This book contains the knowledge and wisdom gained while navigating through and beyond those rough waters.

The Rainbow Bridge

In attempting to create my own way of understanding the world, I have integrated spiritual wisdom from my background and life experiences, which includes the core heart wisdom of the Bahá'i Faith, Buddhism, Christianity, Confucianism, Earth-based traditions, Hinduism, Islam, Judaism, Native American and Indigenous traditions, Sikhism, Taoism, and more.

Throughout most of my life, my father would often talk about koans — questions or statements that initially are contradictory or seemingly don't make logical sense — such as "What is the sound of one hand clapping?" or "What is your original face before your parents were born?" After a series of profound spiritual awakenings and realizations, many mysteries became clear, as though a veil had been lifted. Suddenly, all of the mysterious koans and stories made sense and I was overcome with a deep sense of peace and tranquility, which, thankfully, continues to this day.

In addition, when I was a child, I would occasionally see a car that was plastered with numerous bumper stickers advocating various aspects of social responsibility. These bumper stickers were promoting human rights, the importance of education, saving the whales and dolphins, caring for others in need, protecting the environment, advocating for clean and sustainable forms of energy, promoting equality, having respect for women, demonstrating tolerance (especially when it comes to religion), stopping war, etc. Back then, I would often wonder how much more unified and effective our efforts would be if one bumper sticker could represent all of these causes. I now realize that a bumper sticker of The Rainbow Bridge would do just that.

The Rainbow Bridge

Furthermore, as a direct result of these spiritual awakenings, I recognized that one of my key life purposes is to illuminate the common ground in the world's major wisdom traditions, revealing universal principles that apply to everyone. Thus, in 2001, the first edition of *The Rainbow Bridge* book was born.

The Rainbow Bridge is about inner peace and about world peace. It includes profound esoteric wisdom of the ages in a form that is accessible to everyone regardless of one's belief system, race, age, gender, culture, or background.

The Rainbow Bridge, with each new edition, has represented my current stage of integration of wisdom. It is designed to be simple to read and simple to live. It is designed to assist people who are going through any kind of challenge, for those who are looking for inner peace, and for anyone who is looking for inspiration. The principles in this book can be applied to experience success, happiness, peace, love, and overall bliss in one's life.

Prepare your mind and your heart, as it is our destiny to live in peace and harmony, internally and externally.

What is The Rainbow Bridge?

The name "The Rainbow Bridge" was chosen as the title for two reasons. The concept of a rainbow was used because it is a universal phenomenon seen all across the globe and represents unity — from a multitude of uplifting colors, a single rainbow exists. The concept of a bridge was used because a bridge allows us to get from one place to another, and the destination would often be impossible to reach were it not for the bridge. Bridges always bring different sides together.

To some people, *The Rainbow Bridge* is also known as Humanity's Bridge or The People's Bridge. It is a universal bridge for all of humanity. When someone strives to use the universal principles contained in this book, they are said to be "on The Rainbow Bridge," "on The People's Bridge," or "on Humanity's Bridge."

Describing *The Rainbow Bridge* is a bit like defining love: each person has their own unique perspective. *The Rainbow Bridge* is multi-faceted and means different things to different people. As one becomes more knowledgeable about *The Rainbow Bridge*, it will take on new and expanded meanings, interpretations, and applications.

There are numerous interpretations of the "Rainbow Bridge" around the world. Many people and cultures believe it is a bridge from here to Heaven or from here to God, The Source, The Creator, the

The Rainbow Bridge

universe, or whatever name you wish to use. There is also an ancient Norse legend featured in the movies *Thor* (2011) and *Thor: The Dark World* (2013) that refers to a rainbow bridge — also known as Bifröst — that connects Asgard (Heaven) to Midgard (Earth). The rainbow bridge or tunnel through space-time is also known as an Einstein-Rosen bridge or wormhole, named after Dr. Albert Einstein and his colleague Dr. Nathan Rosen. In 1935, Einstein and Rosen used Einstein's theory of general relativity to propose the theoretical existence of bridges through the space-time continuum.

The Sanskrit term Antahkarana refers to a rainbow bridge, the "bridge of light" or "the lighted way," which is a conduit between our intelligent mind and higher levels of perception and consciousness.

In addition, there are various stories and legends from native and indigenous peoples located around the world, including a legend told by the Chumash people, who originated on Santa Cruz Island. It is an inspiring and uplifting story involving dolphins, and was featured in the movie *Dolphin Tale* (2011).

The Rainbow Bridge is a bridge:

- Between ourselves and our higher selves.

- Between our heads and our hearts, individually and collectively.

The Rainbow Bridge

- Between us and our beloved people and pets that have passed away.

- Between us and all other living beings.

- Between Earth and Heaven.

- Between the physical world and the etheric world.

- Between who we think we are and who we truly are.

- Between the left and right sides of our brain.

- Between the present and the future.

- Between many and One; i.e., it is a vehicle to manifest **E Pluribus Unum** in the physical world. E Pluribus Unum is Latin for "**Out of Many, ONE.**"

- Between religions, races, people, groups, organizations, institutions, and nations. It is a global, universal bridge for **THE PEOPLE.**

- Between our current global economic system, which is based on competition, to a global economic system that is based on partnership, collaboration, and harmony.

- The Rainbow Bridge is a bridge from war to peace, harmony, unity, and prosperity in the 21st century.

The Rainbow Bridge

Due to the variety of ways the Rainbow Bridge can be perceived, it can be viewed as a diamond, with many unique and different facets. No matter from which angle you view the Rainbow Bridge, it leads to and is a desirable destination. Here are a few other ways people perceive the Rainbow Bridge. One of the most well-known rainbow bridges is The Rainbow Bridge for Pets.

The Rainbow Bridge for Pets

The Rainbow Bridge for Pets is a soothing poem and legend that has helped heal the hearts of many pet lovers around the world. It illuminates the permanent connection to their beloved pet, providing comfort that they will meet once again on the other side when they pass on. The anonymously written poem is as follows:

> When an animal dies that has been especially close to someone here, that pet goes to The Rainbow Bridge. There are meadows and hills for all of our special friends so they can run and play together. There is plenty of food, water and sunshine, and our friends are warm and comfortable.
>
> All of the animals who had been ill and old are restored to health and vigor. Those who were hurt or maimed are made whole and strong again, just as we remember them in our dreams of days and times gone by. The animals are happy and content, except for one small thing; they each miss someone very special to them, that special person who had to be left behind.

The Rainbow Bridge

They all run and play together, but the day comes when one suddenly stops and looks into the distance. Her bright eyes are intent. Her eager body quivers. Suddenly she begins to run from the group, flying over the green grass, her legs carrying her faster and faster.

You have been spotted, and when you and your special friend finally meet, you cling together in joyous reunion, never to be parted again. The happy kisses rain upon your face; your hands again caress the beloved head, and you look once more into the trusting eyes of your pet, so long gone from your life but never absent from your heart.

Then you cross The Rainbow Bridge together…

Seen in this way, pet guardians have a permanent connection to their beloved pet.

This same concept applies to people. When a person passes from this life, that person is waiting for you at the other end of the Rainbow Bridge as well, so you have a permanent connection to them and you will meet that person again — once *you* pass on. This interpretation is also in alignment with the Rainbow Bridge as a bridge from the physical world to the etheric world or from our current world to "the other side."

Physical Rainbow Bridges Worldwide

There are a number of physical bridges around the world that are officially named "Rainbow Bridge." Examples include, but are not limited to, the following:

1. Niagara Falls, between Canada and the USA
2. Jinze, China
3. Qinghua, China
4. Yinchuan, China
5. Dortmund, Germany
6. Kochi Kerala, India
7. Hiroshima, Japan
8. Tokyo, Japan
9. The Kyle of Lochalsh, Scotland
10. Seoul, South Korea
11. Penghu, Taiwan
12. Istanbul, Turkey (in process)
13. Oxford, England, UK
14. Tucson, Arizona, USA (in process)
15. Little Rock, Arkansas, USA
16. Berkeley, California, USA (in process)
17. Carmel, California, USA
18. Donner Pass, California, USA
19. Folsom, California, USA
20. Los Angeles, California, USA
21. Sausalito, California, USA
22. Fort Morgan, Colorado, USA

23. Oahu, Hawaii, USA
24. Boise, Idaho, USA
25. Riverton, Kansas, USA
26. Minneapolis, Minnesota, USA
27. Santa Fe, New Mexico, USA
28. Watkins Glen State Park, New York, USA
29. Valley City, North Dakota, USA
30. Grove City, Pennsylvania, USA
31. Beaumont, Texas, USA
32. Navajo Mountain, Utah, USA
33. La Conner, Washington, USA
34. Chippewa Falls, Wisconsin, USA
35. Yellowstone National Park, Wyoming, USA

Rainbow Bridge Stores and Hotels Worldwide

There are also a number of physical stores and at least one hotel around the world that are officially named "Rainbow Bridge." Examples include, but are not limited to, the following:

1. Rainbow Bridge Jewelers in Folsom, CA
2. The Rainbow Bridge Book store in West Palm Beach, FL
3. The Rainbow Bridge Hotel in Yinchuan, China
4. The Rainbow Bridge Natural Food Store in Ojai, CA
5. The Rainbow Bridge store in Nottingham, UK
6. The Rainbow Bridge store outside of Truckee, CA

The Rainbow Bridge

In addition, the Rainbow Bridge has been featured in the world of music. Michael Jackson created a music video for the hit tune "Can You Feel It?" that featured a rainbow bridge, with an introduction that referred to people uniting to build a better world. Jimi Hendrix made a movie titled *Rainbow Bridge* (1972), and a number of Rainbow Bridge festivals have taken place around the world.

As we discover more Rainbow Bridge stores, hotels, movies, festivals, physical bridges and other places, they will be included in future editions of this book. Spontaneously appearing all around the world, The Rainbow Bridge comes from deep within the heart of humanity and is a global phenomenon.

Although there are a multitude of different interpretations, this book focuses primarily on The Rainbow Bridge as a bridge to inner peace and harmony, as well as a bridge to world peace, cooperation, and unity...a bridge to our collective future.

PART TWO

Universal Principles

The Rainbow Bridge

*"That which is hateful to you do not do to others.
All the rest is commentary. Now go and learn."*

— Hillel

The first sentence in the quote above is one of the most important universal principles and concepts that we can apply in our lives. As it turns out, commentary, conversation, dialogue, and diplomacy are of crucial importance in our lives individually and collectively as world citizens living in the 21st century.

Let us now go and learn.

The Common Ground: Universal Principles

The common ground found within the world's major wisdom traditions — also known as universal principles — may be used as guidelines for living our lives to the fullest. They can be used to bring forth deep peace within our own hearts and minds, as well as world peace, harmony, and cooperation.

These are not rigid rules; they are principles that can be utilized during your journey as ideas to be explored; things to keep in mind, and as paradigms to guide you in the process of navigating through the experience that we so confidently call "reality."

The universal principles are not necessarily listed in any particular order, although the first and last principles have been carefully placed as bookends.

The infinity symbols used throughout the book are designed to remind you of your true nature as an infinite being living in an infinite cosmos.

I use the words "God," "The Source," "The Creator," "Higher Power," or "the universe" in an attempt to use universal words for whatever name you feel most comfortable with.

Let us now drop from our heads into our hearts as we step onto The Rainbow Bridge and learn about the common ground, the universal principles…the universal truths that unite people from all walks of life in all corners of the globe. May the bridge image at the bottom of the following pages serve as a reminder that you have stepped onto The Rainbow Bridge. Enjoy your journey!

1
The Golden Rule

Many of us grew up learning that **The Golden Rule** or **ethic of reciprocity** is "Do unto others as you would want them to do unto you."

Perhaps an even more powerful and modern way of expressing this principle is "Do not do to others as you would not want done to yourself." Either way you prefer, this is indeed a cardinal rule that applies to all people everywhere.

"Never impose on others what you would not choose for yourself."

— Confucius

2
As You Think, So It Is

You will manifest what you focus on. Your thoughts, intentions, and expectations about the way something should happen have a direct impact on how it actually happens.

The more time we spend thinking a certain thought, the more likely it will turn into physical reality. Although we don't have spam filters for our thoughts, meditation is a powerful tool that can help us focus only on beneficial thoughts, and meditation can help reduce our thoughts altogether, which can lead to deep inner peace.

When scientists use instruments that measure waves, light appears to be a wave. When they use instruments that measure particles, light appears to be a particle. Life is the same way — we see what we expect to see; we experience what we think we will experience; we see what we believe we will see.

How do you know what you know?
Be careful what you think and believe
Don't believe everything you think
As You Believe, So It Becomes

3
Life Can Have Challenges

Remember that although these concepts are simple, they are not always easy. Seek support and assistance from other people of like mind. Friendship is important. For an excellent treatment of discipline and "getting over" something challenging in your life, please refer to Section 1 of *The Road Less Traveled* by Dr. M. Scott Peck. The basic premise is that once you accept that life can be challenging, you won't be quite so upset when it is. The very moment we accept this truth, the challenge ceases to exist.

Although it can be extremely challenging, sometimes the best thing we can do for ourselves and for others is to accept what is.

> *"Adversity causes some men to break;*
> *others to break records."*

— William A. Ward

4
Life

Most of us have experienced a great deal in our lives…yet most of us are seeking more, something deeper.

Many of us realize during our journey that the more we learn, the less we know. It is when we come upon this realization that true learning can occur, because we become more open to the totality of our experience…not to mention that we begin to learn things we never dreamed were possible.

5
Death

Most of us think we know something about death. However, we often don't really think about it happening to us…and we certainly don't think of it happening to us anytime soon. We feel invincible, so we usually don't deal with the concept of death until it hits us.

However, the sooner we face our own death, the sooner we can become truly free. And the sooner we learn something about death, the sooner we can help those who are dying or help those who are caring for those who are dying.

6
Life After Death

Life follows death.

This is one of the most important concepts in this book. Once we recognize this truth and the relationship of this concept to us as individuals in this lifetime, we learn that death is actually an incredible illusion. Indeed, there is life after death. Life never ends.

The concept of rebirth and resurrection is found in each religion; it is not specific or exclusive to any single religion. Therefore, the concept of being "reborn" or being a "born again" person is a concept that each of us can apply in our lives day to day, minute to minute, and moment to moment.

7
The Path of Heart

Treat everyone with kindness, dignity, respect, and honor. If you can't be positive and inspiring to other people, then withdraw yourself from the situation so that you won't negatively affect them. Always respect the sacred space of others in public and non-public situations.

The Path of Heart has many implications, including extending trust and giving others the benefit of the doubt as much as possible. It's all about opening our hearts ever more deeply to ourselves and towards all other beings.

Be kind to all beings, whether or not you *think* they are living or sentient. Being kind includes not killing or harming other beings.

8
Forgiveness

Forgiveness is of critical importance in attaining inner peace. Forgiveness releases judgment; being forgiving frees your energy so that you can have more of what you want in your life, as opposed to holding on to what you don't want.

When we deeply understand and apply this concept, we discover that it is not only "nice" to forgive others, but *it is in our own best interest* as well. Sometimes we need to apologize in order to be forgiven, so forgiveness and apology often go hand in hand. Forgiveness is a golden gift to both the giver and the receiver. Forgive others, as well as yourself. Let go of judgment and in the process, you will free yourself.

You don't have to agree with or to spend time with others to forgive them.

9
Endless Connections

Everything in life is infinitely interconnected.

When we open our eyes to the wonder and beauty surrounding us, we can begin to see that life is endlessly connected. Social scientists believe there are no more than six degrees of separation between any two people on the planet. This fact is astounding when we think about it. It's similar with situations and events.

This is yet one more reason to release judgments; in the grand scheme, the web of life is endlessly interconnected.

10
Love Your Neighbor

Love your neighbor, friend and foe alike. Love in this sense is not necessarily a feeling; it may be a deliberate action.

There is acquaintance love, fraternal love, familial love, tough love, romantic love, sexual love, and all sorts of combinations and permutations of love. Open your heart. Love everyone, beginning with yourself. It's fun and it shows from the inside out. It's like our heart light is constantly shining and it is contagious.

The rewards come not only to those we love, but also to ourselves, for as we learn and practice love and compassion, we gain levity, lightheartedness and inner peace, which leads to world peace. It's not necessarily easy, but it is simple.

Love yourself and others as if world peace depended on it, because it does (!).

"Love your neighbor as yourself."

— Jesus Christ

11
Respect Your Elders

Respect, honor, and revere your elders. We have a lot to learn from their experiences, wisdom, and knowledge. We must never toss aside our elders as is the predominant behavior and attitude in the United States and elsewhere in the world.

Why do we do this to our elders? More than likely it is simply "because we can." The frequent process of discounting the value of our elders is a completely irresponsible way of utilizing our vital resources. If you cannot see the value for their sake, do it for yourself, for you will be in their place in the future.

Respect our elders, they are our teachers and they are very important members of our human family.

12
Unconditional Love and Compassion

Practice beaming love and compassion to everyone you encounter, espccially people who evoke fear or disdain. People are mirrors for us; if you look into the eyes of another person and see something you think you don't like, it's obvious that you have found a challenge to overcome to accept that person, as well as that part of yourself.

Unconditional love and compassion by definition are not dependent on anything; these are to be given freely. As soon as there are strings or conditions, it serves the giver of love more than it does the intended receiver of love or compassion.

Practice unconditional love and compassion *for others* and *for yourself.* It significantly adds to inner peace and world peace.

"When compassion fills my heart, free from all desire,
I sit quietly like the earth.
My silent cry echoes like thunder throughout the universe."

— Jalal ad-Din Rumi

13
Being of Service

The very act of being of service to others is always empowering. Assisting others with heartfelt, loving kindness connects us with The Source out of which we all arise. It is one of the fastest ways to stop focusing on anything in your life that you think is not going your way. It takes energy to be of service, it takes putting aside your ego and, ultimately, going beyond the ego to a place where there is no separation. Service can be a path to liberation and freedom. It also generates good karma.

"If I am not for myself, who will be for me?

If I am only for myself, then what am I?

If not now, when?"

— Hillel

14
Karma is Cause and Effect

Karma is the law of cause and effect; actions have consequences.

Do not harm others because it will come back to you; "what goes around comes around." If the concept of being nice isn't appealing, be nice for *yourself*, even if you don't want to be nice for the other person's sake. Your next life may be much sooner than you think, and karma can kick in during this same lifetime as well.

15
Love and Friendship

Whether you're in love romantically or whether you're enjoying loving time with friends or family, the benefits of love and friendship are many.

Love in all its forms is the golden key. Love supports you, energizes you, inspires you, illuminates you, expands you, turns you on, and of course, love leads to ever-greater states of peace, joy, and bliss.

Love in its myriad forms is a portal that leads not only to inner peace, but also to a world of peace, happiness, and ecstasy. The more we are able to love ourselves and others, the more others can love us. The more we are loved, the easier it is for us to love others.

Love, Love, Love, Love, Love

> *"Let's be open to the gorgeous colors of the rainbow that make up love and friendship. Let's see the colorful results an ever-loving heart can bring to humanity."*

— Dea Shandera-Hunter

16
A Radiant Spark of Light

Even our smallest actions can make major differences in the lives of others. The power of a smile, the twinkling of an eye and the impact of any individual action may appear insignificant, but it is not. The small things we do benefit others and have untold ramifications for the generation of positive karma in our present and future lives.

Never underestimate the power of one person to make a difference in the world...let that radiant spark of light be you.

"People will forget what you said, people will forget what you did, but people will never forget how you made them feel."

— Dr. Maya Angelou

17
Paradox and Mystery

Expect paradox and mystery on your journey; expect to go beyond your rational mind. Use your heart and mind to go beyond your mind. Go beyond the dualistic worldview of right/wrong, good/bad, above/below, positive/negative. There is a place that exists outside of these realms; this is referred to as going beyond the dualistic world, beyond the dual world, beyond the veil and "out of the matrix."

"Out beyond ideas of wrongdoing and rightdoing,
there is a field. I will meet you there."

— Jalal ad-Din Rumi

18
The Greatest Mystery

Think "out of the box" or better yet, get rid of the box. Connect with something beyond yourself, whatever words you choose to use to describe The Source or your concept of The Source…the source of you, the source of your thoughts, the source of all that exists.

It appears that there are times when The Source chooses to make itself known beyond the shadow of a doubt. During such times, if an individual attempts to deny its existence by the rational mind, tremendous conflict can ensue. We are one and the same as this never-ending, timeless, universal source of consciousness.

19
Find the Silver Lining

Challenges in life can be the very impetus for our growth and liberation. Alchemists refer to this as turning lead into gold in the heat of the fire.

One of the toughest challenges we face is to *find* the silver lining; this is an active process and it can be easy, even if not at first. You have a right to find that silver lining; it is always there for those who seek it. Your openness to it will make it easier to see.

Another helpful thought is to seek out the divinely comedic nature of life, for humor is very healing and can cure many ills.

20
The Present Moment

The only time we have is now; the past is gone and the future has not yet arrived. The present moment is all there is. Learn to live in the present moment, it is precious. If you think about it for a while, you'll see the profound wisdom in this simple concept.

The time is now

Enjoy it

Celebrate it

"Do not dwell in the past, do not dream of the future, concentrate the mind on the present moment."

— Buddha

"As soon as you honor the present moment,
all unhappiness and struggle dissolve,
and life begins to flow with joy and ease.
When you act out of present-moment awareness,
whatever you do becomes imbued with a sense of quality,
care, and love — even the most simple action."

— Eckhart Tolle

21
Through the Looking Glass

One of the most amazing experiences we can have is to discover the non-dual world that transcends our typical experience of life. Returning to the "real world" matrix is not necessarily easy. Once you have stepped through the looking glass, there is no way to unlearn what you have learned.

One of our greatest challenges is to return to the so-called "real world" with the knowledge we have gained. It is vital to bring the gifts of love, compassion, wisdom, and understanding back to your everyday life and to share these gifts with others…to be "in the world but not of it."

"Nothing would be what it is,
because everything would be what it isn't.
And contrary wise, what is, it wouldn't be.
And what it wouldn't be, it would. You see?"

— Lewis Carroll, *Alice's Adventures in Wonderland &*
Through the Looking-Glass

22
Temet Nosce

Temet Nosce or Nosce te Ipsum means "Know Thyself" in Latin, and was inscribed in the Temple of Apollo at Delphi in Greece. This is a very profound statement, for there are things that are completely and totally unknowable by anyone other than yourself.

In the process of learning about ourselves, we attempt to understand why we do the things we do, what drives us, what we believe, what we value, and what is truly important to us. This search for wisdom, enlightenment, and knowing ourselves deeply is critically important to developing a sense of inner tranquility.

During this process of learning, seeking assistance and guidance from others can be very helpful. However, there are times when we must ultimately decide certain things for ourselves no matter what anyone else says — no matter if it is our parents, clergy, experts, psychics, gurus, or anyone else. There are times when looking outside for guidance can actually be detrimental to us — our center is always within. Seek within to connect to your own direct knowledge. You always have the answers within you.

∞

23
Standing Up

Remember that you cannot always please everyone and sometimes the very best thing you can do is to stand up, straighten your back, hold your head up high, and meet your own needs.

This principle is all about standing up to the world to follow your heart, to be yourself, to "march to the beat of your own drum," to be who and what you want to be, and to fully express who you are despite others' potential attempt to suppress you.

The importance of this is shown to us every time we fly in an airplane. The flight attendants always tell passengers to put the oxygen mask on yourself *before* you put the masks on other people sitting next to you — including children and elders. Unless you take care of yourself, it won't be possible for you to fully take care of anyone else.

24
Ask For What You Want

This sounds easy, yet sometimes, the hard part is not asking for what we want, but first knowing what we want. If we don't know what we truly want, it is difficult to ask for it. Sometimes, the hardest part is to learn enough about yourself to know what we truly want…this comes from learning; this comes from self-knowledge; this comes from discernment.

Sometimes, we are afraid to ask for what we want because we are afraid of success, fearful, shameful, have guilt or low self-esteem, etc. Acknowledging these self-sabotaging feelings, if you have them, is the first step in transcending and overcoming them, so that you can ask for and receive what you want from others and from The Source or The Creator.

Become clear about what you want from yourself, from others, and from situations. Then stand tall and ask for what you want.

Ask and You Shall Receive

"Everything you want is out there waiting for you to ask.
Everything you want also wants you.
But you have to take action to get it."

— Jack Canfield

25
Taking Responsibility

In times of stress, uncertainty and doubt, it is easy to give up hope and to think that everything happening to you has nothing to do with you.

In almost all situations, it is more empowering and ultimately more beneficial for you to take full responsibility for your thoughts, feelings, actions, and choices. As you take more responsibility for everything in life, you will feel fantastic because you will develop inner strength and courage. The discipline you gain will also empower and energize you.

26
Dedication and Commitment

Dedication and commitment to oneself, to others, to work, and to life itself can sometimes require deep faith and persistence. Sometimes, things don't come easy, but with dedication and commitment, the forces in the universe converge and deliver.

We can all start with becoming more dedicated and committed to ourselves, in every aspect of our lives. Many people put their time and energies into other people's agendas and in the process, can forget their own lives, families, friends, and colleagues in the process.

Commitment and dedication are especially important when you are looking for the support of other people. If you do not demonstrate serious levels of commitment and dedication, others may understandably lack confidence in you. Part of commitment involves how seriously we take our spoken words. Always do what you say you will do, as this gives others reasons to trust you.

When you demonstrate commitment and dedication in any type of relationship, you will find that others will be much more likely to show you such dedication and commitment.

One definition of "insanity" is doing the same thing over and over again while expecting a different result. A good way around this conundrum is to try new and different approaches, always keeping in mind the goal you have and not necessarily insisting that the one specific path to get to that goal is the only way to get there.

There are many ways to get past an obstacle — over, underneath, around, or through.

"When we feel stuck, going nowhere
— even starting to slip backward —
we may actually be backing up to get a running start."

— Dan Millman, author of *Way of the Peaceful Warrior*

27
Truth and Honesty

It is to everyone's benefit to be truthful, honest, and genuine in your words and in your actions.

There are times when it just seems easier to not tell the truth or to be less than honest. We deny, hide from, deflect, even run away. It is during those times that not telling the truth comes at a cost. When we tell the truth, it is ultimately empowering because we are doing what we know to be right.

Truth and honesty are the right things to do, and are excellent traits to display in all areas of our lives, starting by being honest with ourselves at all times.

28
Timing and Sequence

There are times when we are internally guided to not do anything, to relax, to let things be, and go with the flow. However, there are also times when we are motivated to be in action mode. When stepping into the mode of action, it is important to consider two things with whatever we are doing.

The first is the *timing* of our actions. The second is the *sequencing* of our actions; these are very closely related and yet sometimes it's easy to forget one or both.

Here is an example. Let's say we want to build a simple wooden plank bridge over a river, using nothing but rope and planks of wood. First, we fasten one end of a long rope to one side of the river bank. Then, taking one end of the rope with us, we walk down the river bank, cross the river bed, and walk up the other side of the river bank, securely fastening the rope to this other side.

Next, we fasten one end of a new piece of long rope, go back down the river bank, walk back across the river bed, and walk back up the other side of the river bank, and securely fasten that end near the first rope. Now we have two long pieces of strong rope going across the river.

Starting on the side we're on, we fasten the first plank of wood, then the second plank, the third plank, and so on, until we have reached

The Rainbow Bridge

the other side of the river. Our simple wooden plank bridge will now allow us to walk back and forth across the river.

As far as timing is concerned, imagine trying to navigate across a wildly raging river that is 100 feet deep, while holding one end of a piece of long rope. It would either be very challenging or it would be impossible. From a timing standpoint, it would be best to begin the process of building the bridge before the river has little or any water in it, if possible...build the bridge before the river swells.

As far as sequencing is concerned, we need to first ensure that the ropes are going back and forth across the river before we can fasten the wooden planks to it. We would also want to fasten the wooden planks to the rope starting on one end of the river bank, as described above, as opposed to attempting to fasten the first plank halfway across the river.

Timing and sequencing are two dynamics that can be easy to forget. Anyone who has tried to assemble a barbecue grill or piece of furniture knows how easy it is to accidentally skip a step or make a mistake, which can create long delays in the process.

29
Not "If," But "How" and "When"

When you are attempting to manifest something you desire in life, it is helpful to act with a deep belief that you will in fact see the desired outcome.

Don't wonder *if* you will be able to do something — wonder *how* you will do it, wonder *when* you will do it, and wonder *under what circumstances* it will happen.

If you haven't been given the consciousness to know *how* and *when* something will happen, then act with deep conviction, a deep knowing, that it will happen and it will indeed happen (refer to the **Acting "As If"** principle (#44)). The importance of this concept cannot be overstated, for answers and solutions are sometimes provided only after we move forward with deep faith.

Acting from a sense of knowing that you will create what you want increases the probability of actually attaining it, whatever it is.

There are times when we don't always get exactly what we're looking for; we get a variation of what we wanted. During such times, it is important to manage our expectations, be flexible, and be OK with the outcome understanding that we are getting what we "need" versus what we "want." During such times, this principle is closely connected with the **Surrender** principle (#31).

∞

30
Balance and Moderation

Seek balance and moderation in all areas of your life to move closer to deep inner peace.

In some circumstances, it's to your advantage to use not just moderation, but extreme moderation.

Imbalances are not always easy to see...they can be our "blind spots." Stepping back and reflecting on our lives can often provide a greater and higher perspective.

31
Surrender

There are times in the dream of life when things don't appear to turn out the way we wanted them to. There are times when it is clear that the outcome was out of our control and there is nothing else we can do. During such times, it is important to be flexible and to "surrender" to the situation. Indeed, sometimes it is the only choice we have.

In such situations, we can gracefully surrender to the situation as it is, or we can struggle and suffer, kicking and screaming along the way. We gain an incredible amount of energy and experience less angst and stress as well. When we have less stress in our lives, it is easier to gain insight, creativity, and overall excitement.

Although this might be easier to say than to do, it's a very important concept to remember along the journey of life.

32
Meditation and Sitting

Sometimes the best thing you can do is to meditate, to "just sit," or to "just be." Sometimes, just sitting, being quiet, and contemplating is deeply centering. There are many ways to do this, including a large number of different meditation techniques. *Just relax and be with yourself.*

Sometimes, when we are sitting or not sitting, getting out of our heads and into our hearts is the best thing — and often the only thing — we can do for ourselves in certain difficult periods of time.

Sitting can lead to surrender, to acceptance, and to deep inner peace.

33
Dynamics of the Ego

We often hear about people who have "big egos." We read that the ego is something to overcome, something to slay, something to get rid of. However, I believe the best way to think about the ego is that it can be transformed and that it is an integral and useful part of our whole being. One of our goals is to transform the ego from being self-centered to being other-centered.

Being centered on meeting the needs of others is another way of saying that we are being of service. Seen in this light, it's not bad to have a transformed "big ego" because it makes us more effective at manifesting things that are for the good of humankind.

Another way of noticing the transformation of the ego is when we begin to identify with the unity of all life. At this point, we realize that our notion of separation is an illusion, and that we are actually completely at one with everything. Transcending our notion of being a separate, ego-based individual is a profound transformation that occurs in our lives when we are open to experiencing it. When we recognize that we are actually no different than The Source, our ego either seems like a small and insignificant part of the vast universe or we realize that we are one with it. Indeed, nothing is the same as everything.

34
Expect Changes

Expect the unexpected and have no fear. Things change; be willing to release your grip, your control, and your attachments.

There are very few guarantees in life. However, death and change rank near the top, so it only makes sense to come to terms with the fact that life is not permanent and that it will change.

Times of change can be painful, upsetting, and deeply disappointing. Everything that happens in life is for our own development as individuals and collectively, no matter what happens and no matter how painful or destructive it is. Seen in this way, change is actually our friend in that The Source or universe is helping us to awaken ourselves, to expand our awareness and to discover what true freedom is.

Learning to deal with change is a very profound way for us to learn to live in the present moment and to experience the bliss and perfection that is always here.

This principle is closely connected with the **Surrender** principle (#31).

35
Don't Take Things
Personally

Occasionally, things happen in life that have nothing whatsoever to do with us and yet we ascribe meaning to these situations as if it did.

Sometimes, we're at the grocery store, a clerk is rude to us, and we react. The clerk could be going through a rough time in his or her life. Rather than thinking "How could they be so rude to me!" don't take it personally and just let the person have their bad day. When we don't take things personally, we can often see situations more clearly, more objectively, and with less frustration.

36
Peaks and Valleys

Vital energy is often experienced in peaks and valleys, and in ebbs and flows, which are a natural part of life.

Another way to describe these fluctuations is to say that vital energy shifts or is transformed at times. It is important to know that energy doesn't disappear; it just gets transformed into different forms of energy. When energy isn't appearing in an abundant fashion, conservation can be helpful.

37
The Darkness

Sometimes, we have to experience the pain of darkness and suffering in order to more fully appreciate the light. Sometimes, we have to enter the hot and dry desert in order to more fully appreciate the deliciousness of the oasis. Sometimes, we have to taste bitterness in order to fully appreciate sweetness. Sometimes, we must experience the Dark Night of the Soul.

The dark is thus the catalyst that can facilitate a greater appreciation for the gift of light.

"A rainbow appears in your own tears
if you'll look to The Light."

— Pastor Rick Warren

38
Moving On

Reactions and emotions such as fear, anger, jealousy, pride, etc., are all within your control. Other people can try to push your buttons, but the buck stops with you when it comes to what you think, what you say, what you do, and what you feel. This may not be easy, but it is always in your control. Although it might seem harsh, we sometimes have to "just get over it" and go on with our lives when it comes to dealing with the circumstances that arise in life.

This principle is closely connected with the **Surrender** principle (#31) and the **Expect Changes** principle (#34).

"Our problems and our pain don't
necessarily go away,
but we can take the focus off of them
by engaging life and appreciating the moment
that life brings us
with every single breath that we take."

— Jim MacLaren,
from *The Good Life* by Jesse Dylan

39
Don't Panic!

There are times when the weight of the world seems heavy on our shoulders. At times, the discoveries we make and experiences we have are shocking and difficult. Sometimes, we can become exhausted, overwhelmed, and even disoriented. Indeed, our very sense of reality can become challenged. This is exactly what happens when the mental, rational, and intellectual mind is pushed beyond its limits.

During times such as these:

- Let go of panic
- Let go of fear
- Breathe deeply
- Seek out the support of others
- Trust the universe

"Fear invites you to play, for it can't play alone.
Alone, it has nowhere to go and nothing to do."

— Bill Froehlich,
Filmmaker and Co-author of *U R The Solution*

40
Breathe

Breathe! Seriously! Sometimes, it is incredibly helpful to just stop and take deep breaths. Focus on your center, find the spot within where peace resides, and breathe into that space. If you think you can't find any kind of inner peace, focus on where you think the peace is, where it could be, or where you want it to be.

If all else fails, don't think about anything — just take deep breaths and feel the energy and life force coming into your body.

*"Breath is the link between your body,
your spirit and your mind."*

— Sri Sri Ravi Shankar

41
Trust

Have trust and keep the faith no matter what you *think* is happening. Don't get hung up on differences between trust, faith, etc…the base concept is the same. Keep your mind, body, and soul focused on whatever it is that you want.

No matter how long you feel you have been struggling or suffering, trust the universe and keep the faith…there is light at the end of the tunnel.

The **Dedication and Commitment** principle (#26) is important with respect to the issue of trust.

"Where there is faith, there is harmony, unity, and love."

— Amma

42
Let Go of Fear;
Become Fearless

As Franklin D. Roosevelt once said, "The only thing we have to fear is fear itself." This is a truly profound statement.

Depending on the circumstances, fear is completely natural and can be a powerful ally. However, sometimes, our fears are based on false assumptions (**F**alse **E**vidence **A**ppearing **R**eal). It is this type of fear that is to our benefit to eliminate or reduce. Courage is when we act in the face of fear.

Reducing our fear or acting in the face of it is not always easy. Seek out others who you can learn from, who support you, who empower you, who inspire you, and who uplift you. Friendship and love are important in overcoming fear.

"Courage is being scared to death...and saddling up anyway."

— John Wayne

43
Focus on What You Want

Our minds are extremely powerful and cause whatever we focus on to manifest in physical form. In order to manifest a desirable outcome, it is important to focus on the outcome we wish to manifest versus the outcome we wish to avoid. If we spend an inordinate amount of time thinking about everything we *don't* want, we have that much less time and energy to focus on what we *do* want. Focus on what you want, and then work hard to make it happen.

This is closely related to **The Power of Thought** principle (#45).

"Determine that the thing can and shall be done,
and then we shall find the way."

— U.S. President Abraham Lincoln

"You are never given a wish without also being given the power to make it true. You may have to work for it, however."

— From *Illusions*
Richard Bach

44
Acting "As If"

If you're not sure about your ability to do or have something, act "as if" something were already true — this is a very powerful way to achieve success. Act with a deep conviction that the reality you desire already exists, and it will increase the probability.

For example, if you are participating in a sports competition and feel strongly that you will win the event, you will pull out all the stops: you will exercise long and hard, you will watch your eating habits, you will get plenty of sleep, you will be 100% focused, etc. You act "as if" you know deeply that you will win. You do what it takes to win the race, knowing all the while that you are going to be successful.

On the other hand, if you don't really think you will be successful, then you may cut corners while exercising, you may eat extra snacks, and you may not focus your mind as intently as you otherwise would. In the latter case, you are not acting as if you will be successful. In the former case, acting as if you were already successful increases the chances of attaining success.

This principle is strongly related to the **Not "If," But "How" and "When"** principle (#29).

45
The Power of Thought

Our thoughts and intentions are extremely powerful. Our thoughts are the seed of physical manifestation.

Our minds are similar to radio stations; we can "tune in" to many different thought forms. It is up to us to decide what stations we want to tune into. Our minds not only receive information similar to radio stations, but they also transmit information. Remember that we have the power to "change the station in our mind" if we don't like the thoughts.

Be conscious of the thoughts you have — anything is possible with focused attention, intention, and action.

Focus, Focus, Focus
Concentrate
Don't Necessarily Believe Everything You Think

"If you can conceive it in your mind,
then it can be brought to the physical world."

— Bob Proctor

46
Interpretation

Mastering interpretation is of great importance. The experiences we have in our lives do not always have inherent meaning; we create meaning based on how we interpret the things that happen. It is helpful to make an effort to always use the most empowering and uplifting interpretation for yourself and others.

For example, if one knows that our energy naturally ebbs and flows, one is less likely to interpret the fluctuations as something we have brought upon ourselves. Ebbs and flows, peaks and valleys are a natural and organic part of life.

Another example of the importance of interpretation — what does the word "jihad" mean? It means *struggle*. Everyone must deal with the *internal* struggle between the ego, id, and superego; the *internal* struggle between the heart and mind; and, of course, the *internal* struggle between the ego and The Source.

Practice makes a big difference.

47
Perspective

In order to arrive at the most inspiring, uplifting and empowering interpretation of any given situation, it is helpful to approach it from a different perspective. Often, when we can view a situation from someone else's perspective, we can see the situation in an entirely new way.

Try to understand different perspectives and you'll be amazed at what is revealed to you.

Practice makes a big difference.

"The greatest discovery of all time is that a person can change his future by merely changing his attitude."

— Oprah Winfrey

48
Information and Wisdom

Our ability to understand our lives, to form the most inspiring interpretations, and to have the most useful perspective is dependent upon the information and wisdom to which we have access.

For those of us who are fortunate enough to use the Internet, it provides unparalleled doorways to information, knowledge, and connections to people worldwide.

Stay tuned into and informed about what is happening on the Internet; the global brain and heart awakening in cyberspace. Information, knowledge, and wisdom are ever-present and available for those who seek it out. Finding and developing wisdom can be done in many ways, especially through introspection and meditation.

49
Discernment

From *Webster's Revised Unabridged Dictionary* (1996):

Discernment \Dis*cern'ment\, n. The power or faculty of the mind by which it distinguishes one thing from another; power of viewing differences in objects, and their relations and tendencies; penetrative and discriminate mental vision; acuteness; sagacity; insight; as, the errors of youth often proceed from the want of discernment.

Some types of discernment come only through experience, over time, and with knowledge of one's self. What is discerned by you, may not be discerned in the same way — or at all — by others. Look within to discern knowledge directly.

This principle ties in with the **Information and Wisdom** principle (#48).

50
There Is Always More

Sometimes, we can have awakening or enlightenment experiences that significantly expand our consciousness. This can lead to the blissful experience of feeling like we are at one with the cosmos; where the inner becomes the outer; where the macrocosm becomes the microcosm, where above becomes below and below becomes above, etc. At that point, we can feel like we know everything there is to know. This can sometimes be dangerous because we can have secondary and tertiary awakenings where we realize that there is more to learn.

There is no end to consciousness, information, knowledge, and wisdom. This realization can either be daunting or it can give rise to tremendous inner peace as we stay in the present moment.

"A human soul may be thought of as an opening through which Infinite Energy is seeking a creative outlet."

— Emmet Fox

51
Follow Your Heart

We normally guide ourselves by using our rational mind. While the mind can be a powerful tool, when we are faced with difficult decisions, it helps to remember that we have an entirely different faculty for helping us make decisions: our heart, our intuition. I believe that we can almost never make a wrong decision when we follow our hearts. We may make what we *think* are mistakes from time to time, but even these situations lead to learning, personal growth, and a deeper sense of knowing who you are and what is important to you.

If you are ever in doubt whether to follow your mind or your heart, follow your heart for direct knowledge.

52
Music — The Universal Heartbeat

Music is a universal language that unites people from all walks of life, all cultures, and in all corners of the world. Music soothes and heals the heart, body, mind, and soul. Music helps bring us to an inner place that is outside of time and space, and music brings us closer to peace, joy, and bliss.

"Music is the voice of all humanity, of whatever time or place. In its presence we are one."

— Charlotte Gray

"Music washes away from the soul the dust of everyday life."

— Red Auerbach

53
Mystical Love

"The way of love is the great way.

When we love, we want to love totally, completely. But when we love, loving a person or falling in love with God, the Absolute, our love fails us. We say, "I will love you forever."

How quickly we get caught up in other events, other interests. Non-love is our ordinary state.

To learn the way of love means to train in eternal love, ceaselessly loving. To keep loving, like breathing itself — never being distracted from this involvement in love.

Then we enter into a new state — then we experience mystical love. This is an entirely new state of human evolution."

— Venerable Lama Kunzang Rinpoche

54
Express Appreciation

Express gratitude and appreciation for what you have. Don't take anything for granted.

Whatever you focus your attention and intention on will expand. When you spend time being appreciative of what you have, that area of your life will grow and increase.

If you feel that you're not getting everything you want in life, think of the things you don't get that you don't want (seriously!).

Gratitude is the deepest form of prayer.

55
Listen to Others

Often, when we are trying to listen to others, we spend time thinking of what we are going to say next, which gets in the way of our completely listening to the other person. Active listening is a skill that may require effort, but it is well worth the time and effort. Learn to truly listen, for then you will be heard.

"If we are speaking, we are not listening or learning anything to add to our sum of knowledge. This is why the first step to effective listening is to stop talking!"

— Ken Fracaro

"The most basic of all human needs is the need to understand and be understood. The best way to understand people is to listen to them."

— Ralph Nichols

56
Share With Others

Learn to give freely, for then you will open yourself to fully receive.

Very often, giving or sharing what we ourselves have been previously denied or what we have little of can be very healing. What you give will be returned to you at least tenfold, and not necessarily in the way we expect.

Give and share what you can, when you can, while you can. You will feel great.

"Do not turn away a poor man...
even if all you can give is half a date."

— Muhammad

57
Patience

We all know that patience is a virtue. It is often easy to be patient when we know *why*. Given the *reason*, we feel confident that our patience will lead to the result we wish to have. When we don't know *why*, we need to be patient or we question whether we will achieve our desired outcome. This is when patience can be much more difficult and even more important to apply and practice.

For example, we all know we need to wait for a flower bud to open. We know that if we try to open the petals of a flower before it is ready, we will destroy the flower and not see the beauty we were seeking.

Another example is the real-world miracle of a caterpillar transforming into a butterfly. The metamorphosis process includes a period of time in which the caterpillar is no longer a caterpillar, and not yet a butterfly; it is in a state of disintegration and chaos, yet also a state of reorganization and integration.

Due to lack of patience, we might be tempted to open the cocoon before the butterfly is ready to emerge. However, being tightly wrapped in the cocoon is a very important part of the birth process. The pressure of the cocoon, and the attempt to emerge from it, pushes the blood to the ends of the wings and helps the butterfly fully develop. If we were to open the cocoon before the butterfly is ready to emerge, the butterfly would be harmed and would not be able to fly. Knowing this process, it is easier to be patient.

In both of these situations, if there is lack of patience and outside pressure is exerted, damage will most likely occur. So one of our most important lessons is to be patient *even if we don't know why* or if being patient will lead to the outcome we desire.

"How does one become a butterfly?

You must want to fly so much
that you are willing to give up being a caterpillar."

— From *Hope for the Flowers*
by Trina Paulus

This principle must be carefully balanced with **The Present Moment** (#20) and **Surrender** (#31) principles, and using the **Timing and Sequence** (#28) principle, remembering that it is always beneficial to be patient, relaxed, and non-judgmental in the present moment.

58
No Permanent Character Judgment

Do not judge others; view others as mirrors to learn more about yourself and to practice compassion.

Most of us constantly make judgments of one kind or another, especially about other people. It's best to not judge at all. However, if we do judge, at least consciously make them temporary judgments. It's not helpful to permanently put a person into a certain category and label them: they could have had a bad day, a bad month, a bad year, or a bad decade (seriously!). Just as it's not useful when you are permanently labeled by someone else, it's not useful to do this to others, or to yourself.

"If you judge people, you have no time to love them."

— Mother Teresa

"Hate the sin, love the sinner."

— Mahatma Gandhi

59
Live and Let Live

Learn to allow, for then you will be free.

Sometimes, we need to agree to disagree. Even in disagreement we can be in agreement. Respect and love can prevail even when disagreement is present.

As we allow others to "just be," we learn how to appreciate them exactly as they are. To the extent we do this for others, inner appreciation for ourselves flourishes. As we let others have the freedom to be who they are, we gain the freedom to be who we are. Freedom to be who we truly are leads to inner peace. Freedom to let others be who they are leads to world peace.

This principle must be carefully balanced with **The Path of Heart** (#7), **Balance and Moderation** (#30) and other principles, always consciously seeing others as another aspect of ourselves to love, accept and integrate.

You don't have to agree with others in order to let them be; to let them live.

60
Life is a Dream

Things are not always as they appear; life is an illusion…life is like a dream and life *is* a dream.

We can accelerate the awakening process through the conscious practice of lucid dreaming. Lucid dreaming is the experience of knowing you are dreaming while you are still dreaming at night. This not only allows you to affect the outcome of your dreams, but lucid dreaming also shows us that what we focus on (including what we fear) can often be what shows up in our dreams…and in our lives.

Just like we can become lucid and wake up when we're dreaming at night, *we can also become lucid during the daytime dream of life.*

"The universe is dreaming itself awake."

— Paul Levy

Notes Regarding The Use of Universal Principles

Focusing on Common Ground

The importance of deliberately focusing on common ground when seeking harmony between you and other people, as well as between different people and groups, cannot be overstated. For many of us, our minds have been trained from an early age to find differences as opposed to finding commonalities. Focusing on what is common — the common ground — is an important and valuable skill to develop and fine tune.

As far as the common ground in the world's major wisdom traditions, some people believe that some religions are mutually exclusive or diametrically opposed to one another. Although this may be true for some specific technical details, it is not true for entire religions or groups of people. The reason is because there is a huge continuum of beliefs within each wisdom tradition, and everyone who believes in a specific tradition doesn't interpret everything in exactly the same manner. In addition, there are people in every religion who hold extreme views and interpretations. When we deliberately and consciously focus on what is common between ourselves and others, we find that we are not so different after all. When we focus on what unites us, we are immediately at greater harmony within ourselves as well as with others, in our homes, communities and workplaces.

I would like to mention one important example of the powerful practice of focusing on common ground because it is of such vital importance for our own peace of mind, as well as for helping bring about a peaceful, more harmonious world for ourselves and for future generations.

It is a common practice to deliberately not discuss politics (or religion!) when we're in the workplace. Each of us can probably think of people we work with who have widely divergent political views than our own. By consciously avoiding the topic of politics, we are forced to think of what we might have in common with the other person when we have a conversation with them. As a result of taking part in conversations that don't divide us, we can often find something to appreciate in the other person. While we might not be best buddies with the other person, at least we can learn to be in harmony with them. Learning how to have harmonious relationships with others, especially others we might not understand, is of critical importance in experiencing greater peace within ourselves. It is also important in terms of helping to bring about a better world for all of us.

"There exists far more common ground between the world's great religions than most people think. By concentrating on shared values and truths we can discover an opportunity to break down barriers of hate, misunderstanding and cynicism to foster brotherhood, tolerance and peace."

— John Scheinfeld,
Director/Producer of *Heaven*

Faith

The subject of faith can be complex and at the same time, paradoxically, it can be very simple. I suggest thinking about faith in terms of having faith in what you *need*, not necessarily what you think you *want*. Be open to receiving gifts from the universe even if they might not be exactly what you had in mind. There is a great story that powerfully illustrates this point.

Once upon a time, there was a man who was sitting on his roof after a huge flood. As he sat on the top of his roof, a person in a canoe paddled up to the front of his house and yelled, "I'm here to help, hop in and I'll carry you to safety." The man on the roof said, "No thank you — I have faith, I'll be just fine."

A short while later, the police arrived in a motorboat and told the man, "The waters are rising, come down and we'll help you get to dry ground."

The man said, "Thank you, but I have faith. I'll be safe up here."

The motorboat left and the water levels continued to rise. After a few more hours, a rescue helicopter hovered directly above the house and lowered a rope ladder. The rescue team told the man to climb up the rope ladder and they would fly him to safety. The man said, "I've prayed and I don't need your help because I have faith."

The Rainbow Bridge

A short while later, the water rose above the roof, the man drowned, and he went to Heaven. Once in Heaven, he demanded, "I prayed for you to save me, I had faith. How could you do this to me?"

The Creator then said to the man, "I sent you a canoe, then a motorboat, and then a helicopter. What more did you expect?!"

"Don't miss out on a blessing because
it's not packaged the way you expect."

— Anonymous

Change, Death, Rebirth, and Life

Critically important throughout this book is the concept that life changes; it is impermanent. Universal principles found in all of the world's major wisdom traditions help us navigate the waters of change, death, rebirth, and life.

The first editions of *The Rainbow Bridge* were subtitled *Universal Book of Living, Dying and Dreaming* because they deal with the subjects of living, dying, and dreaming in a non-dogmatic way that includes and honors all of the world's major religions and schools of thought. Even though the sub-title was changed in the third edition, the foundational content remains the same.

Many people have heard of *The Egyptian Book of the Dead* or *The Tibetan Book of the Dead*. It may come as a surprise to know that a large number of books have been written about living and dying, all with similar sounding titles. Here are just a few others, in alphabetical order:

- *The American Book of the Dead*
- *The Celtic Book of Living and Dying*
- *The Christian Book of the Dead (The Divine Comedy)*
- *The Hindu Book of the Dead*
- *The Islamic Book of the Dead*
- *The Jewish Book of Living and Dying*
- *The Maya Book of the Dead: The Ceramic Codex*

The Rainbow Bridge

- *The Pagan Book of Living and Dying*
- *The Tibetan Book of Living and Dying*

> *"Death would not be called bad, O people,*
> *if one knew how to truly die."*

— Guru Nanak

An Internet search will turn up a surprisingly large number of books with similar names; further exploration from various perspectives is encouraged.

In conjunction with other sources such as the Bible, the Koran, the Torah, the Bhagavad Gita, the Tao te Ching and others, these sources contain profound information on what it means to live and die in this so-called "reality."

So what's all of the fuss about life and death? Why are so many people talking about life and death — especially death? Why is it considered to be so important to know all about death — to supposedly prepare ourselves and our loved ones for the afterlife? It's hard enough to live in this reality while focusing on life let alone learning anything about death. And therein lays the secret.

An open secret.

While you read this book, please expect things to be simple rather than complex. Expect to deal with paradoxes (mysterious and seemingly contradictory situations). Life and death are filled with mystery and paradox.

The information in this book has been passed on through the ages in different ways by all of the world's major religious, spiritual, and philosophical schools of thought. *The Rainbow Bridge* is a 21st century articulation of the wisdom of the ages.

The concepts in this book may contain multiple layers of meaning. You may want to read *The Rainbow Bridge* multiple times, for your ability to understand and appreciate new interpretations will expand infinitely over time.

Synchronicity

Synchronicity is the regular occurrence of "meaningful coincidences"; the incidence of events that seem to be meaningfully related to our lives and life experiences.

The more we are drawn into the dream of life, the more we become conscious of the incredible and always exciting synchronicities that constantly happen all around us. To the extent that we understand what synchronicity is and make a point to be open and on the lookout for it, we will see and experience synchronicities with greater frequency. The experience of life becomes ever more magical, more blissful, and more filled with awe and wonder.

Decisions

We almost always make the right decisions based on the information in front of us. The challenge is usually that we lack accurate and/or complete information whether we realize it or not. Therefore, the key to making decisions that lead to positive outcomes is *to ensure that we are using current, accurate, and complete information.*

Through earnest conversation, we can gain new perspectives and interpretations. In terms of ensuring that we access and utilize the best information, open conversation is of critical importance in solving interpersonal problems, as well as the world's problems.

As we will soon discuss in greater detail, one of the reasons the world is in a state of massive disarray is because we lack a smoothly functioning global operating system and, therefore, we are not using all of the information we have access to. When we are able to fully apply universal principles to all of our decisions, the world will become completely different.

Many decisions can be made by following two down-to-earth rules of common sense that are highlighted in Richard Maybury's book *Whatever Happened to Justice*:

1.   "Do all you have agreed to do."

2.   "Do not encroach on other persons or their property."

The Rainbow Bridge

In addition to all of the universal principles we have explored, the simple and straightforward concepts of being responsible and having respect for all others is common sense. When it comes to international affairs, *following universal principles is common law based on common sense.*

The quality of our lives and of all humanity rests in the decisions we make, individually and collectively. Let us choose to use all of the information we have at our disposal, including universal principles in every area of our lives. To exercise full responsibility, we must use all of our knowledge, wisdom, and consciousness. Let us choose to live out our greatness by fully engaging ourselves — it is indeed our destiny to live in peace and harmony worldwide.

Learning

One of our challenges along life's journey is when we learn something really profound, because it can lull us into a sense of feeling like we know everything there is to know. Then, when we least expect it, we will get another lesson that teaches us that there is more.

Just like trying to find our way out of a labyrinth or maze, we sometimes return to situations and lessons we thought we had already mastered...and then we learn a new paradigm or a better way. Our ability to focus our mind, attention, and intentions are good examples of lessons we can return to repeatedly.

There are times in life when we feel we are "in school." To the extent that you are hanging out with a group of people and you feel that you are "in school," learning, this can be a good sign. It is important to note that there are many schools of thought, and that exploration can add clarity to your learning and growing experiences.

The seminar of "life" on Earth is something we all share in common as fellow world citizens — we're all in it together and new things to learn are always available to us.

The Rainbow Bridge

Putting It All Together

While reading this book, you may have been frustrated at times because some of the principles seem to contradict others. Going within to find the answers and "thinking out of the box" can be helpful in putting the pieces of the puzzle together.

Here is an example. Walking The Path of Heart calls for treating everyone you meet with love, dignity, honor, and respect. Another principle we've discussed is standing up and meeting your own needs. Other principles we've covered are being honest, truthful, and genuine. How do all of these fit together? What if we meet someone we really don't like? Shouldn't we meet our own needs, be truthful, be authentic, and let them know what we *really* think?

> *Being nice to someone you don't like isn't*
> *being two-faced, it's being mature.*

The key to answering this question is to know whose interests are being met when you make a decision to take such an action. If you encounter someone who rubs you the wrong way and you still respect, honor and treat them well, you are meeting their needs and you are sending out positive energy to the world. In a small, but definite way, you are making the world a better place.

If you insist on telling that person how horrible they are and how they should change their ways, you are meeting your own needs. That person (no matter how right *or* wrong you are) will not be uplifted. One way to get around this conundrum is to take yourself away from that person — to love them from a distance — and later talk it over with someone you are close with to get it out of your system in a genuine way by speaking your truth.

> *"When the choice is to be right or to be kind,*
> *always make the choice that brings peace."*
>
> — Dr. Wayne Dyer

There are times in life when practicing the concepts, such as the one described above, takes more energy out of you than you have or want to give. Love is an active process that requires time and energy. It is important to take care of yourself and to meet your own needs. The only person who can truly know what decision to make in such situations is you.

Learning to strike a balance between meeting your own needs and meeting the needs of others can be a major life challenge and learning opportunity.

You may find it to be very helpful to read books, to see movies, to seek the advice and counsel of others, and to see how other people are handling similar situations. At the end of the day, though, all of your answers can be found within. Seek within, look inward to discern your own inner truth and don't stop until you experience inner peace, joy, and bliss.

Trust your intuition, follow your heart, and follow your bliss.

PART THREE

Inner Peace

*"He who lives in harmony with himself
lives in harmony with the universe."*

— Marcus Aurelius

The Rainbow Bridge

*"When meditation is mastered, the mind is unwavering,
like the flame of a lamp in a windless place."*

— Krishna

A Bridge to Inner Peace

We all have a desire for peace, happiness, and joy in our lives. To the extent that we can experience greater levels of peace within ourselves, we can then more easily be at peace with others.

The Importance of Introspection

When it comes to inner peace and tranquility, the importance of introspection and self-reflection cannot be overstated.

The subject of inner peace and well-being is the subject of my first book, *The Pieces of Our Puzzle: An Integrated Approach to Personal Health and Well-Being.* The book, based on the importance of introspection, provides a holistic synthesis of the world's major schools of psychology.

It is helpful to imagine that living our lives is similar to putting together a complex jigsaw puzzle. When assembling a complicated puzzle, we start by looking at the big picture before the individual pieces, as it helps to understand visually what we're putting together. Our lives are similar: it helps to understand the big picture...we all want to have inner peace, happiness, and deep fulfillment.

With this as the basis for putting together our own magnificent puzzle, we introspectively look at the psychological aspects of our lives: our thoughts, feelings, behaviors, past history/environment, current environment, and relationship to The Source. Piece by piece, we contemplate, evaluate and meditate on the various aspects of our lives, with the goal of creating a single, harmonious, and unified whole.

In addition to looking at the different psychological aspects of ourselves, we can perform the same type of introspection with the universal principles. We can look at each principle to see how it fits given the unique circumstances present in our lives and in the world. Our lives are constantly changing, so it is natural to find that some universal principles are more important at certain times.

Searching within our hearts and minds to understand who we are, why we do what we do, who do we wish to be, what is important to us, what are our priorities, what do we wish to leave as our legacy? These are all critical questions to reflect upon in our quest to "know thyself." Using the universal principles to guide our thoughts and actions, and carefully balancing when and how we use them, can help lead us to greater states of inner peace and joy.

Creating a Bridge to Your Future Self

A very powerful way to create a bridge to inner peace is the exercise of creating a bridge to your future self. Close your eyes and in your mind's eye, imagine yourself in the future. Envision yourself filled with peace, harmony, and joy. Imagine what it feels like to be living a life filled with peace and harmony, filled with deep bliss physically, mentally, emotionally, and spiritually. See yourself in the future, and make a decision that you are that person.

It helps to also imagine a bridge of multi-colored light from your current self to your future self. As you go about your daily routine, imagine that you are using universal principles with every step you take. With each passing moment, you are getting closer to being your future self. As you intentionally utilize universal principles in your life, you are increasing your sense of inner peace and you are becoming more of the future self you are imagining.

Meditation

A powerful and ancient method to increase your sense of inner peace and tranquility is through the practice of meditation. Meditation is a deep and profound practice that can help you find your center at any time, especially during challenging times. There are innumerable ways to meditate, to "just sit" or to "just be." These include visualizations, reciting of mantras, meditations that focus on one's breathe or heartbeat, meditations that focus one's attention on an object such as a flame, mindfulness meditation, Transcendental Meditation (TM), Kundalini meditation, movement meditation, and more.

The Rainbow Bridge

*"One of the reasons so many people are suffering from stress
is not that they are doing stressful things,
but that they allow so little time for silence."*

— John O'Donohue

Meditation and Prayer

The difference between meditation and prayer is an age-old question. Nonetheless, it is often said that praying is talking to God or The Source (often with a request), whereas meditating is the act of listening. Meditation practices are designed to still our minds and move us into greater states of inner peace and tranquility. However, meditation and prayer can also be combined in a powerful hybrid approach to not only cultivate a sense of inner calmness, but to also usher in desired change. The power of our minds is astonishing, and by combining visualization with focused intention and prayers/requests to the universe, we can manifest powerful changes in our lives. This section includes a few samples of hybrid meditations/prayers that I describe as meditation. I call these meditations and not prayers to acknowledge that when communicating with The Source, listening is more important than speaking.

The Importance of Practice

In virtually every area of our lives, we must sometimes do things repeatedly in order to learn, improve, and excel. As the saying goes, "practice makes perfect." The concept of practice applies to developing our inner selves and reaching a sense of inner tranquility by searching within, understanding ourselves, and meditating.

The Rainbow Bridge

We cannot expect to meditate just once to experience a deep sense of inner peace: it is much more effective when we practice the art of self-reflection and meditation on a consistent, routine, and sustained basis. Although this may seem like common sense, it bears noting because people sometimes wonder how many times they need to meditate before they will see results. The concept of practice is so central to meditation that people frequently refer to their meditation routine as their "meditation practice." Making self-reflection and meditation a regular part of your daily routine will greatly assist in the development of inner peace and tranquility.

Preparing to Meditate

It is best to choose a quiet place where you will be comfortable and not be disturbed. Turn off your phones and other devices. Wear loose-fitting clothes and handle any restroom needs before you begin. If you enjoy incense, then light some. Turn off the music and dim the lights. Many people will fall asleep if they attempt to meditate while laying down, so it is best to sit in a comfortable chair, preferably with a straight back. Begin by closing your eyes and taking a few deep breaths. Feel your body relaxing from your head to your toes.

Sample Meditations

This section includes a few examples of special Rainbow Bridge visualization meditations that can help facilitate inner peace, as well as world peace, no matter what is going on in your world or the world at large.

The Rainbow Bridge

Sitting/Walking/Running Meditation

As you are sitting, walking or running, imagine a beam of multi-colored light — a Rainbow Bridge — connecting your head, your heart, and your entire body to The Source. Imagine this is a permanent connection, imagine you are not alone, nor can you ever be, and imagine receiving love, information, knowledge, wisdom, and energy from The Source at the other end of The Rainbow Bridge.

Breathing Meditation

Imagine a Rainbow Bridge connecting your head, your heart, and your entire body to The Higher Power. Imagine that every breath you take in is vibrant energy and refreshing air coming into you from the other side of The Rainbow Bridge. Notice how good it feels and how relaxed you become when you perform this simple, yet profound, act of breathing. Imagine that every time you exhale, you exhale air and energy to the other side of The Rainbow Bridge, establishing an even deeper connection with every breath you take in and let out.

Energy Meditation

As you are sitting, imagine a beam of golden-white light with rainbow-colored shimmering sparkles coming from the universe and entering your body from the top of your head. This sparkling, golden-white light travels down through your head, neck, spine, and then through the base of your spine to the center of the Earth.

The Rainbow Bridge

Imagine that this Rainbow Bridge of light connects, cleanses, and energizes every part of your body. It also connects you to your Higher Power while firmly grounding you to Mother Nature and to planet Earth.

Meditation Between Your Head and Heart

Close your eyes and imagine a golden-white ball of light in the center of your head. Now imagine a golden-white stream of light, shimmering with the various colors of the rainbow, going from the center of your head to the center of your heart. As this stream of light lands in your heart area, imagine a ball of golden-white light forming around your heart. Your head and your heart are deeply connected.

Meditate on the strong connection now formed between your head and your heart. See energy flowing back and forth through this Rainbow Bridge of light to and from your head and heart. Imagine how this bridge connects and integrates you. Know that this bridge exists and helps you become at peace and at one with yourself and with all of humanity.

Meditation for Two or More People

Close your eyes and imagine a golden-white ball of light in the center of your chest. Now imagine a stream of golden-white light, shimmering with the colors of the rainbow around the edges, going from your heart to the heart of the other person(s) you wish to connect with and vice versa. Know that this Rainbow Bridge of light and love connects your hearts, minds, and souls. Feel how this bridge of light connects you to the other person(s) and know that it is real.

The Rainbow Bridge Trinity Meditation

This meditation helps connect us to other individuals and/or groups of people. By envisioning a Rainbow Bridge connecting our heart to someone else's heart, another Rainbow Bridge connecting our head to another person's head and a third Rainbow Bridge connecting our eyes to another person's eyes, we create a very powerful connection to the other person(s). We might wish to perform this meditation with someone we love, or to perform this meditation with someone we don't get along with to help bridge the gap between the two of you. This meditation can be used prior to conversations that might be challenging, as it creates a triple bridge (heart, head, and eyes) between you and the other party. This is a powerful meditation that often produces profound results.

Meditate with Beings on the "Other Side"

This meditation is a modified version of The Rainbow Bridge Trinity meditation. By connecting in this way with people or pets on the other side of The Rainbow Bridge, not only do we feel more connected to that person or pet, but we can also merge with that being's consciousness. Merging with another's consciousness is a powerful way to experience being connected and at one with the universe, and perhaps gaining the precious realization that everything else is an illusion.

The Rainbow Bridge

Meditating On Your Vision, Future, and Desired Outcome

This meditation is another version of the previous two meditations. In this version, sit comfortably with your back straight, breathing naturally, fully feeling the relaxation and perfection in the present moment. Imagine the future you would like to have for yourself, your loved ones, your community, and for all of humanity. Be specific and just let it flow in an inspiring, uplifting, and empowering manner. Rather than focusing on what you *don't* want, envision the desired outcome and feel how you will feel when you have achieved the desired result. Know that it will happen. Then let it go, as if letting go of a helium-filled balloon that catches the wind and rises to the heavens.

Lover's Rainbow Bridge Meditation

You can do this meditation with or without your beloved sitting next to you, although it is even more powerful if you are physically together. Close your eyes and take a few deep breaths. Each of you should imagine a golden-white ball of light in the middle of your chest. See a powerful beam of golden-white light, shimmering with the colors of the rainbow around the edges, emanating from your heart and entering the heart of your partner. Take a few deep breaths and experience and enjoy how good it feels to be connected heart-to-heart.

Now imagine a golden-white ball of light in the middle of your head, and see a bright beam of golden-white light sparkling with the colors of the rainbow emanating out of your head and gently entering the head of your partner and vice versa. Relax and take a few more deep breaths in unison.

Now that the connection of your heads and hearts is completely activated, imagine hundreds, then thousands, then millions, then billions, then trillions, and then quadrillions of beams of multi-colored colored light going to and from every cell, atom, quark, and neutrino in your body to and from every cell, atom, quark, and neutrino of your partner. Know that you are completely connected, completely merged, completely at One with one another, at peace with yourselves and with the world, in harmony, and in deep bliss.

If your true love hasn't shown up in your life yet, it is also powerful to do this meditation with the intention of meeting your beloved, as it will begin the process of your souls merging and help call them into your life.

Meditate the Helix Nebula Into Your Heart

Some people have heard of the amazing Helix Nebula, also known as "The Eye of God" (you can see a picture of the Helix Nebula on the back cover). The Helix Nebula is a trillion-mile-long tunnel of dust, rocks, and cosmic matter pointing to our planet. This phenomenon can serve as a meditative tool to ponder the meaning of life, the purpose of our existence, and for connecting to the vast, open-ended nature of the universe. We can also utilize the existence of the magical Helix Nebula to imagine love, wisdom, information, and energy coming from the Helix Nebula into our heart and body, filling every strand of our DNA with powerful new energy and wisdom. We can envision being "plugged into the universe" by the very act of imagining being connected in this way via a shimmering Rainbow Bridge of light.

Meditate Your Intentions/Prayers into the Helix Nebula

This meditation is a modified version of the meditation above. In this version, you can imagine Rainbow Bridges of light connecting you and your entire body, mind and soul to the Helix Nebula, right into the Eye of God. When doing this meditation, imagine that you are connected directly to The Source. Being directly connected to The Source by a Rainbow Bridge of light into and through the Helix Nebula, you can send prayers and intentions from your heart directly into The Source. This is an extremely powerful way to meditate, pray, and to express appreciation for the miracle of life.

Circumpolar Rainbow Bridge Meditation

The late Mayan scholar and global advocate for systemic change, Dr. José Arguelles, created a beautiful "Circumpolar Rainbow Bridge Meditation" to help manifest The Rainbow Bridge to Peace. Although some people might find it to be complex and difficult to visualize, here is the short form of his powerful meditation:

"Visualize yourself inside the Earth's octahedron crystal core (with two red and white sides on top, and two blue and yellow sides below). In the center of this core is an intensely blazing point of white light. An etheric column extends North and South from the blazing center to the tips of the octahedron.

The Rainbow Bridge

Coiled around the etheric axis like two strands of DNA, are red and blue flux tubes. In the crystal core are four time atoms. A red time atom is strung on the northern axis, and a blue one on the southern. The gravitational plane of the octahedron emanates horizontally from the center point. Along this plane are two more time atoms, a white and a yellow one, which turn like paddle wheels making a counterclockwise motion around the center.

Now visualize that from the center of the crystal a great stream of multicolored plasma-filled light flows along the axis toward both of Earth's poles, shooting out from them to become two rainbow bands 180 degrees apart. As Earth revolves on its axis, this Rainbow Bridge remains steady and constant, unmoving.

Next take the whole vision of the Rainbow Bridge around the Earth and place it in your heart. Imagine the two streams of rainbow light rushing through your central column, shooting out from above your head and beneath your feet to create a Rainbow Bridge around your body. Now you and the Rainbow Bridge are one. The Rainbow Bridge of world peace is real. Visualized by enough people in a telepathic wave of love, The Rainbow Bridge will become a reality."

Simplified Rainbow Bridge/Antahkarana Meditation

As mentioned in the beginning of this book, the Sanskrit term Antahkarana refers to a "bridge of light," "the lighted way," the "central light column," the "central channel," or the Rainbow Bridge. These are all interchangeable terms for this powerful conduit between our intelligent mind and higher levels of perception

and consciousness. There are advanced meditations and visualizations one can use to build your personal Antahkarana and at the same time, the planetary Antahkarana.

Here is an extremely simplified, introductory meditation practice that can help build your Rainbow Bridge of Light, your personal Antahkarana.

Step 1: Send a Bridge of Light from You to Your Soul

Imagine in your mind's eye a strand of light, a bridge of multi-colored light emanating upward from the top of your head to your soul, located above your head. Imagine sending rays of light connecting you to your soul, starting from the top of your head and moving upward. You can envision this as an act of reaching out and knocking on the door of your soul to seek greater connection. This act of connecting with your soul is a request and your soul will respond accordingly, opening up and eventually sending more love, light, energy, and consciousness. Do this as often as possible.

Step 2: Envision a Bridge of Light from Your Soul to The Source

After some time, imagine another bridge of multi-colored light, a Rainbow Bridge, extending from your soul to The Source or The Creator. Continue to see this stream of multi-colored light pulsating from your soul to The Source. Repeat as often as possible.

Step 3: Envision a Bridge of Light from The Source to Your Being

Imagine a bridge of multi-colored light coming from The Source to yourself, down into the top of your head. Repeatedly see and feel this stream of energy and higher consciousness coming from The Source into the top of your head, through your body, and down to the center of the Earth. Dedicated and sustained daily practice will grow this bridge of light in a very powerful way. As you build your own personal Antahkarana, you are contributing to the building of the planetary Antahkarana as well, playing an important role in the manifestation of world peace.

Step 4: Building and Widening the Rainbow Bridge/Antahkarana

Each time you perform this profound 4-step meditation practice, it builds a bridge of light to higher consciousness. Each time you perform this exercise, it builds more strands, filaments or channels of light, and gradually the number of strands of light increase, become wider and merge together. As the light channels become more numerous and larger in size, this bridge of light has more "bandwidth." Therefore, through diligent practice, you will continue to receive increased amounts of light, energy, consciousness, perception, and wisdom flowing into you from The Source and from your soul.

Advanced Study and Practice

The previous vastly abbreviated meditation practice is not intended to replace the much more advanced practices designed to build and widen the Rainbow Bridge, the Antahkarana. For more detailed descriptions of advanced esoteric practices designed to build the Antahkarana, feel free to explore the work of Alice Bailey, Josephine and Norman Stevens (aka Two Disciples), Dr. Ronald Tiggle, Dr. Joshua David Stone, Rick Prater, Aart Jurriaanse and Benjamin Creme, among others. This powerful technique of building your Antahkarana is a profound way to bring about a greater sense of peace and harmony, to increase your connection to The Source, and to help build the planetary Antahkarana at the same time.

The Rainbow Bridge

The Rainbow Bridge World Peace Meditation

Sit in a quiet place and go comfortably inward. Just breathe and experience the sensation of your breath entering and leaving your body. Close your eyes and imagine you are part of a large group of people around the world, billions of people, each who are imagining a Rainbow Bridge connecting their heart, mind and soul to their higher power, and connecting their heart, mind and soul to every other person and being in the world, connecting businesses to businesses, connecting institutions to institutions, and connecting nations to nations.

Envision large waves of energy running to and through you and into the other people around your family, your town, your state, and your country to all other local towns, states, and countries. Now imagine looking at the Earth from far away in space and see it covered by a large web of electric, pulsating rainbow-colored light.

Imagine people all around the world, dancing in the streets, celebrating wisdom and success and peace — inner peace and world peace.

Imagine how you are an integral part of a much larger whole, feel how completely connected you are and how you are at One with everything all around you. In your mind or out loud, speak the words "Peace begins with me," "Peace," "Unity," "Oneness," and then proclaim "And so it is."

PART FOUR

World Peace

*"To accomplish great things,
we must not only act but also dream;
not only plan, but also believe."*

— Anatole France

The Rainbow Bridge

*"We must learn to live together as brothers
or we will die together as fools."*

— Dr. Martin Luther King, Jr.

A Bridge to World Peace

The world is filled with beautiful stories of miracles, amazing good works being done by many people and organizations, and breakthroughs that continue to take place in every field of endeavor. At the same time, the world is plagued with multiple simultaneous global crises ranging from widespread poverty, to war and crime, to global economic instability, to climate crises, to natural disasters of biblical proportions, and much more.

"Our world faces a true planetary emergency."

— U.S. Vice President Al Gore

Clearly, there is an urgent need to resolve our problems in order to decrease suffering and to help usher in a new age of peace and prosperity. The time for peace is at hand — it is time for us to put aside our differences and make way for unity amidst our diversity, to create bridges of understanding, and to work with one another side by side for peace and a better world for all.

The Rainbow Bridge

The world around us is a reflection of our individual and collective minds. Therefore, world peace will arise when a tipping point is reached, and where great numbers of people are experiencing increased levels of inner peace in their own lives, regardless of what may be going on around them. This is why inner peace is so important not only for ourselves, but for the world. Each of us has a responsibility to make it a priority to find peace within — for all of our brothers, sisters, and children in the world.

By reaching our own inner peace, we can be at peace with those who are close to us. Peace and joy start within ourselves, and then extend to our families, friends, cities, states, nations and finally, to the entire world.

As we feel a greater sense of peace and harmony within ourselves, we find that many things become easier, not the least of which is receiving new information and clarity about our lives. This includes receiving increased knowledge about how to utilize universal principles to help create a bridge to the future. Even though we may not yet have all of the answers we seek, we can take the first steps and go from there. As Thomas Carlyle wisely stated, "Go as far as you can see; when you get there you will be able to see farther." Along the same lines, Martin Luther King, Jr. astutely observed that "You don't have to see the whole staircase, just take the first step."

After 13 years of consciously living by the universal principles described in this book, I continue to receive "downloads" of new information regarding how to use universal principles in concrete, practical, and useful ways to help bring about greater levels of inner peace, as well as world peace. The additional information regarding how to help create a bridge to world peace is contained in this section of the book. Similar to the way we can create a bridge to our future selves as individuals, collectively, we can also create a bridge to our future world — a world of great peace, harmony, and prosperity.

We will now continue to learn how universal principles and our expanded consciousness can be used to help bridge the gap between war and peace in the 21st century — a bridge to world peace.

The Rainbow Bridge

"Any sufficiently advanced technology
is indistinguishable from magic."

— Arthur C. Clarke

Life and Conscious Evolution
in the 21st Century

We live in a completely infinite, totally open-ended universe. With the advent of the Internet, literally billions of people around the world can be linked and communicate with one another instantaneously. This miraculous capability, along with further advances in technology, means that we have the ability to consciously focus our attention and intention to mutually co-create anything we want to create, individually and collectively. There is no limit when we marry technology with universal principles and heart-based, positively-focused intentions.

Life in the 21st century is fundamentally different than any other time in our history. It is beneficial to remind ourselves that we live in a new era because it really makes a difference in how we think, what we expect and what we believe will unfold now and in the future. A major aspect of life in the 21st century is the conscious evolution of our species.

The Rainbow Bridge

"You and I are essentially infinite choice-makers.
In every moment of our existence, we are in that field of all
possibilities where we have access to an infinity of choices."

— Dr. Deepak Chopra

One of my favorite thoughts is "In a world of infinite possibilities, it is irresponsible to be pessimistic." We owe it to ourselves, our children, and to future generations to be fully conscious humans knowing that it is in our power to take part in co-creating a new reality that is heart-based and filled with cooperation, collaboration, partnership, unity, harmony, reconciliation, inner peace, and world peace. I have witnessed humanity moving in this direction for many years and it excites me as I see more and more of it everywhere I look.

The Rainbow Bridge

"What we appreciate, appreciates."

— Lynne Twist

The Law of Attraction in the 21st Century

The Law of Attraction, as featured in the works of New Thought pioneers as well as "The Secret," is a fundamental law or great truth of the universe. However, the way the concept is often shared has been narrowly focused on how individuals can manifest what they want in the physical world (such as cars, houses, boats, perfect partners, etc.) by the power of the mind and emotions. There are a number of important ingredients missing and you'll see there are many more secrets than just one.

The Law of Attraction can be used in a much more expansive manner to serve humankind and the planet. I believe the next-generation understanding and use of the Law of Attraction and next stage in our evolution will occur when millions of people use the Law of Attraction to collectively co-create a better world that works for everyone. With the power of the Internet, we have the ability to collaborate with one another, person by person and group by group, with shared and highly focused intentions, to co-create a positive and sustainable global future for all generations to come.

The Rainbow Bridge

In the future, The Rainbow Bridge's Earth Communications Center will be launched, a socially responsible international communications infrastructure and social network that will facilitate and enable such communications and co-creation/collaboration.

A very exciting development starting to take hold is the "Department of Peace" concept. It's rooted in the understanding that whatever we focus our attention and intention on is what we manifest, and that if we spend some of our resources on a cabinet-level Department of Peace, we will significantly accelerate the peace-building and peace-maintenance process.

In the U.S., this process is being spearheaded by The Peace Alliance and the Student Peace Alliance, where local grassroots chapters have been formed in all 50 states. Internationally, a global movement for Ministries of Peace and Departments of Peace is being spearheaded by Global Alliance for Ministries and Departments of Peace. Although a strong military might be needed for *defense*, it is time we start to spend our time, energy, and trillions of dollars focusing on peace. The efforts to build Ministries and Departments of Peace will go a long way toward bringing us closer to our collective goal of world peace.

The Rainbow Bridge

*"Not only is another world possible, she is on her way.
On a quiet day, I can hear her breathing."*

— Arundhati Roy

Earth's Global Operating System
in the 21st Century

The key purpose of a computer operating system is to equitably distribute the resources of the system. Just imagine if a computer had no operating system; any program could secure and utilize all of the CPU power, all of the hard drive space, all of the memory, and all of the peripheral devices. This would make it nearly impossible for any other program to run very efficiently.

Today's world is a highly complex, completely interconnected and interdependent system and yet the world does not have a single, smoothly functioning, sustainably-designed global operating system[1]. Therefore, it is no surprise that the world's resources are not being distributed equitably, why there is so much income disparity, and why there is so much widespread poverty and violence in the world.

It is clear we have massive global problems that require global solutions. It is sensible to recognize the need for some type of new global system of governance — a global operating system — and to

---

[1] The best we've got is The United Nations, but many major systemic changes are still needed for it to be a fully operational, non-biased global operating system, a topic covered in the next section.

The Rainbow Bridge

do what it takes to create a system that works for everyone. If we can send people to the moon and back in spacecraft, if we can send an enormously powerful telescope into space to record some of the most spectacular images ever seen, if we can send a spacecraft to Mars — which is a minimum of 35 million miles away — and land a vehicle that drives around the surface and sends photographs and data back to us here on Earth, we can certainly architect a global operating system that honors life in all of its precious diversity, and ensures the equitable distribution of resources for all people regardless of where they live.

During my conversations about this subject over the years, I've noticed that people invariably have fear and trepidation about the idea of any form of global governance. This probably comes from the fact that many governments currently do not adequately serve the needs of their People. Many are fearful about any single person or group having too much power. These concerns assume that the implementation of global governance takes the form of existing governmental models. We don't need to be bound by our past models or ways of thinking; we can create an architecture for any system we want for The People. We just need to consciously focus on what is needed and to be aware of what didn't work well in the past and continually improve upon it, always remembering that all peace and justice causes are always about serving The People.

When architecting a smoothly functioning global operating system, it is best to design a system that is of, for, and by The People. Governments are meant to work for The People, not the other way

The Rainbow Bridge

around. Let us never forget that in a democratic republic, when The People lead, the leaders follow and take action.

To this end, I envision the need for an International Magna Carta ("Great Charter") that would spell out the fundamental human rights of The People worldwide. This would build on and improve upon the important work of the past, including but not limited to the original Magna Carta created in 1215, the Declaration of the Rights of Man and of the Citizen created in 1789, the U.S. Bill of Rights created in 1791, the First Geneva Convention created in 1864, the Universal Declaration of Human Rights created in 1948, and the Earth Charter, officially launched in 2000.

"My tenure will be marked by ceaseless efforts to build bridges and close divides."

— United Nations Secretary-General Ban Ki-moon

As we put our heads and hearts together to engineer a new global operating system that works for all of us, many people will be pleasantly shocked because they will learn that not only is there more than enough to go around for everyone, we actually live in a completely abundant universe. Once we modify energy companies into people-serving, non-profit organizations or utilities, research on alternative clean energy technologies will dramatically increase until we find a clean and reliable alternative to the use of petroleum. Fortunately, there are many technologies that are highly promising including using the sun, water and air as fuel, transforming air into clean water (which can be used for drinking or for fuel), etc.

The Rainbow Bridge

We have such an exciting future ahead of us, but we must take concerted action to come together to turn the possible future into the actual future. It is of critical importance that we create a global operating system for the 21st century that honors the sanctity of all life on the planet, and that helps us address the multiple, simultaneous global crises we have the opportunity to resolve.

The Rainbow Bridge

*"Is there any way of delivering mankind from the menace of war? ...
As one immune from nationalist bias, I personally see a simple way
of dealing with the superficial (i.e. administrative) aspect of the
problem: the setting up by international consent of a legislative and
judicial body to settle every conflict arising between nations..."*

— Dr. Albert Einstein

Empowering the United Nations

In the aftermath of World War II, after some 50 to 80 million people
died a group of visionary international leaders created the United
Nations, "to save succeeding generations from the scourge of war."
Since its founding, the U.N. has brought humanitarian relief to
millions in need and helped people rebuild their countries from the
death and destruction of armed conflict. It has promoted human
rights, fought apartheid, protected the rights of children, challenged
poverty, promoted democracy, raised the visibility of critical
environment and gender issues, spearheaded efforts to help rid the
world of the horrors of nuclear weapons, and promoted social
progress and better standards of life and freedom. According to Dr.
Shashi Tharoor, former United Nations Under-Secretary General of
Communications and Public Information, the U.N. has helped end
more civil wars through mediation since 1945 than in the two
previous centuries.

Tharoor has also pointed out that for the average person, the U.N.
has made their lives better in ways they might not even imagine. The
next time you fly on an international flight, you can thank the U.N.,

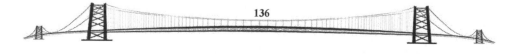

The Rainbow Bridge

because it is their International Civil Aviation Organization that makes international travel possible. Anytime you listen to an international radio station or watch an international television station, you can think of the U.N. because it is the U.N.'s International Telecommunication Union that coordinates usage of radio and television frequencies. Similarly, the U.N.'s Universal Postal Union makes it possible to send mail to another country or to buy a foreign product. These are just a few things provided by the U.N. that we might not know about or might take for granted.

Despite the important and valuable contributions made by the United Nations since it was inaugurated, there are a number of issues that require updating to best serve humanity during the 21st century and beyond. Chief among these issues is the Security Council, the most powerful branch of the U.N., which is the only U.N. body with the authority to issue binding resolutions to member states. It is composed of just five permanent members (China, France, the Russian Federation, the United Kingdom, and the United States) and each has veto power, as well as ten non-permanent rotating members without veto power. While this group of five nations reflected the power structure of the world at the end of World War II in the 20th century, it needs to be upgraded to reflect the geopolitical realities of the 21st century.

The U.N. General Assembly is one of the six major organs of the U.N., and is the only one in which all members have equal representation. However, delegates to the U.N. are appointed by their respective nations. Therefore, the average citizen has no voice in the way the U.N. operates. A proposed addition to the U.N.

system on the table is a United Nations Parliamentary Assembly, or United Nations People's Assembly (UNPA), which would allow for direct election of U.N. Parliament members by citizens all over the world.

Fortunately, the need for change at the U.N. is widely known and discussed. In 2005, former U.N. Secretary-General Kofi Annan created a detailed report titled *In Larger Freedom* that discusses the previously mentioned issues and more, along with specific proposed solutions. As of 2007, U.N. Secretary-General Ban Ki-moon continued this agenda, which focuses on oversight, efficiency, integrity, and ethics. In addition, other proposals were put forth by the G4 nations (Brazil, Germany, India, and Japan), as well as the Uniting for Consensus group. In 2011, Secretary-General Ban Ki-moon announced the formation of a U.N. Change Management Team (CMT) focusing on streamlining and improving the efficiency of this very important world body.

Albert Einstein summarized some of the above topics in an open letter to the U.N. General Assembly in 1947, two years after the end of World War II and the founding of the U.N. Here is part of his letter:

> *"As a matter of fact, the United Nations is an extremely important and useful institution provided the peoples and governments of the world realize that it is merely a transitional system toward the final goal, which is the establishment of a supranational authority vested with sufficient legislative and executive powers to keep the peace.*

The Rainbow Bridge

The present impasse lies in the fact that there is no sufficient, reliable supranational authority. Thus the responsible leaders of all governments are obliged to act on the assumption of eventual war. Every step motivated by that assumption contributes to the general fear and distrust and hastens the final catastrophe. However strong national armaments may be, they do not create military security for any nation nor do they guarantee the maintenance of peace.

Security is indivisible. It can be reached only when necessary guarantees of law and enforcement obtain everywhere, so that military security is no longer the problem of any single state. There is no compromise possible between preparation for war, on the one hand, and preparation of a world society based on law and order on the other.

Every citizen must make up his mind. If he accepts the premise of war, he must reconcile himself to the maintenance of troops in strategic areas like Austria and Korea; to the sending of troops to Greece and Bulgaria; to the accumulation of stockpiles of uranium by whatever means; to universal military training, to the progressive limitation of civil liberties. Above all, he must endure the consequences of military secrecy which is one of the worst scourges of our time and one of the greatest obstacles to cultural betterment.

The Rainbow Bridge

If on the other hand every citizen realizes that the only guarantee for security and peace in this atomic age is the constant development of a supranational government, then he will do everything in his power to strengthen the United Nations. It seems to me that every reasonable and responsible citizen in the world must know where his choice lies."

Einstein, in no uncertain terms, communicates the need for international law and order secured through a supranational system of governance. In addition, he makes the profound point that whether we wish to live in war or in peace, it is a decision that each of us needs to be aware of and to make.

Regarding the issues with the Security Council, Einstein continues:

"The time has come for the U.N. to strengthen its moral authority by bold decisions. First, the authority of the General Assembly must be increased so that the Security Council as well as other bodies of the U.N. will be subordinated to it. As long as there is a conflict of authority between the Assembly and the Security Council, the effectiveness of the whole institution will remain necessarily impaired.

The Assembly, in view of these high tasks, should not delegate its powers to the Security Council, especially while that body is paralyzed by the shortcomings of the veto provisions. As the only body competent to take the initiative boldly and resolutely, the U.N. must act with utmost speed to create the necessary conditions for international security by laying the foundations for a real world government."

The U.N. is the closest thing to a global operating system the world has ever seen, and continues to make significant contributions that make the world a better place. It makes perfect sense to put forth serious attempts to upgrade this important international organization for the benefit of humanity, and to save succeeding generations from the scourge of war.

The Rainbow Bridge

"Universal responsibility is the best foundation both for our personal happiness and for world peace, the equitable use of our natural resources, and, through a concern for future generations, the proper care for the environment...."

— Tenzin Gyatso, H.H. the 14th Dalai Lama

The Global Commons

The term "global commons" is typically used to describe international, supranational, and global resource domains in which common pool or common property resources are found. Global commons include, but are not limited to, the earth's shared natural resources, such as the deep oceans, the atmosphere, and outer space.

A large and growing number of people around the world are beginning to recognize that natural resources are to be shared, they don't belong to any nation or group of people — they belong to all of us. A strong case could be made that these resources don't even belong to us, but rather that we are the caretakers, the guardians of the Earth's precious resources. As conscious global citizens, we must protect and equitably share these vital resources.

The global commons is comprised of three types of resources/goods:
1. Public goods, which are managed by governments
2. Private goods, which are managed by corporations
3. Common goods, which belong to and are managed by The People

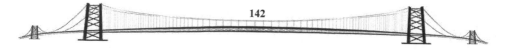

The Rainbow Bridge

The concepts of stewardship and trusteeship that are behind the global commons allow us to think about our planet in fundamentally different ways with the goal of creating a better world for everyone. One such example is an initiative called the Global Marshall Plan, or Global Commons Plan.

Global Marshall Plan/Global Commons Plan

The idea of a "Global Marshall Plan" was first published in 1992 by Al Gore in his book *Earth in the Balance: Ecology and the Human Spirit*, shortly before he was elected Vice President of the U.S. Gore deliberately chose the name to recall the historical Marshall Plan (officially the European Recovery Program, ERP) that was implemented after World War II. The Marshall Plan was an American initiative that provided economic support to rebuild European economies and help rebuild war-shattered regions. It also provided markets for American goods, and created stronger trading partners for the U.S. The initiative was named after Secretary of State George Marshall, received bi-partisan support, and is generally credited with helping Europe rise from the ashes of war. The phrase "equivalent of the Marshall Plan" is often used to refer to any wide-scale rescue program.

There are initiatives underway to help create a "Global Marshall Plan," including, but not limited to one put forth by Al Gore mentioned above, the Global Marshall Plan Initiative (globalmarshallplan.org) and one proposed by the Network of Spiritual Progressives (spiritualprogressives.org).

The Rainbow Bridge

Some people object to the word "Marshall" because it evokes images of martial law. Global Marshall Plan initiatives can also be considered Global Commons Plan initiatives.

In the third edition of this book, I proposed a Global Commons Unification Project. This plan includes working with other Global Marshall Plan organizations to bridge them and create a single unified plan. At its core, the plan involves creating a pool of funds where resources are distributed and all decisions are made at the global level using universal principles. The Rainbow Bridge Global Commons Unification Project would help create jobs and stimulate local, national, and international commerce and friendship through various community-development programs such as food, water, and energy projects; housing and community center projects; educational projects; transportation, bridge, and road-building projects; a project to create an International Magna Carta; and more. Our $3 trillion long-term plan (minimum of $150 billion per year for at least 20 years) applied at the global level would help create order out of the currently unstable global economic system. It would create a global network of financial and cultural bridges and treaties between people from all walks of life, religions, races, cultures, organizations, and nations.

Development of a Commons-Based Economy

The global commons also provides us with a framework for understanding how to address the issues and risks in our global financial system through the development of a commons-based economy. Approaches being researched and advanced include but are not limited to commons-based peer production and the

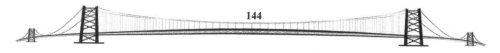

commons-based economic system being developed by James B. Quilligan and the Global Commons Trust (globalcommonstrust.org). These efforts are at the forefront of modern thinking to create an economic system for the 21st century that would serve all of humanity in a way that meets the needs of many more people than the current economic system does today.

The Global Commons Plan/Global Marshall Plan initiatives and efforts to create a commons-based economy are of critical importance toward creating a new global operating system that will serve the needs of the people, the environment, and all beings living on this planet. These initiatives are quite promising and deserve serious consideration and support, especially when we imagine the possibility of creating a hybrid system that combines the best of both models.

We are here on Earth for a short period of time and one of our responsibilities is to leave our surroundings better than we found them, in particular, the global commons. This is a fundamental premise in many organizations such as the Boy Scouts, Girl Scouts, 4H Clubs, and countless other groups around the world. It is also common-sense wisdom found in the hearts and minds of many people worldwide. The concept of leaving something better than we found it creates the possibility that we step outside of ourselves, out of our normal ways of thinking and being, to a more conscious and compassionate way of viewing the world and its inhabitants. World citizens working for the common good are guardians, stewards, and protectors of the global commons and everything it encompasses.

"The earth is but one country and Mankind its citizens."

— Bahá'u'lláh

World Citizenship

As we have seen while exploring the need for a new, smoothly functioning global operating system, we must step beyond our personal, as well as local, regional, and national issues and take a global view when attempting to resolve our most pressing challenges. It is critical to appreciate the fact that global problems require global solutions.

This leads us to the critical concept that we are all world citizens on this small planet, even though we might not yet view ourselves this way. We all live in a village, city, or town. At the same time, we also live in a county, region, or state. In addition, we live in a country. Likewise, every single one of us lives on this planet so it only makes sense that in addition to our more local way of identifying ourselves, that we would also consider ourselves to be world or global citizens.

It feels like the world is getting smaller every day. It will be very helpful for every one of us, no matter where we live, to adopt the idea that we are all world citizens, and to realize that our identification as world citizens doesn't preclude us from belonging to any city, region, state, or country.

∞

The Rainbow Bridge

"I like to believe that people in the long run are going to do more to promote peace than our governments. Indeed, I think that people want peace so much that one of these days governments had better get out of the way and let them have it."

— U.S. President Dwight D. Eisenhower

Jubilee and Debt Forgiveness

Although it might seem unrealistic, the practice of a "Jubilee" is an ancient tradition that has been practiced for hundreds of years to help ensure balance and harmony. It also celebrates life, forgiveness, and redemption. Traditionally, the Jubilee involved a release from indebtedness and all types of bondage. Prisoners and captives were set free, slaves were released, debts were forgiven, and property was returned to its original owners. One of the benefits of the Jubilee was that both the land and the people were able to rest and be replenished. The activation of this "reset switch" essentially restored balance and benefited everyone, just as a rising tide lifts all boats. All wisdom traditions promote the idea of providing relief to those in need. Given the state of our unbalanced world and given the unacceptably high number of people around the world who are in need, perhaps a carefully planned Jubilee is just what we need to help restore balance, communal harmony, and peace.

If you have ever played the game "Monopoly," you know there is a point in the game where one person has a lot of houses, hotels, property, and money. After a while, it is literally impossible for

The Rainbow Bridge

others to catch up, much less to win. In a very real way, our world is similar to a giant game of Monopoly in the sense that there are a very small number of people who control the vast majority of the world's resources, and the majority of people are just trying to survive.

> *"Global poverty is a powder keg that could be ignited by our indifference."*
>
> — U.S. President William J. Clinton

According to Oxfam, the richest 1% in the world own almost half of the world's wealth. In addition, according to the United Nations, roughly half the people in the world struggle to survive on less than $2 per day. Even if we take into consideration currency differences and barter arrangements, the enormous gap between those who have and those who do not have is widening and is grossly out of balance. It is horrifying to know that according to the United Nations more than 16,000 children starve to death every day. Since it takes roughly 3 weeks for a person to slowly starve to death, there are roughly 336,000 children in the process of starving even as you read this sentence. A Jubilee would help pave the way for an entirely new global system to emerge where every world citizen has the right to life, liberty, and the pursuit of happiness. Many details would need to be worked out to ensure a smooth and positive result, but a well-planned Jubilee and "reset switch" could very well help restore balance and harmony in the world.

The Rainbow Bridge

*"We are the people the world has been waiting for...
and now is the time to act as one."*

— Adapted from
A Message From The Hopi Elders

A Bridge in Time

As we traverse the Rainbow Bridge together, with the collective intention of creating a positive, sustainable future that works for the greatest number of people in the world, we are traveling across a bridge in time together. We navigate this bridge together from our present moment to a time in the future — whether that time is 10 seconds from now or 10 years from now. The terrain we have under our feet is the common ground found in the world's major wisdom traditions; as we have discussed, this foundation is also known as universal principles. The Rainbow Bridge is therefore a bridge to the future: our future of peace, harmony, unity, and prosperity.

"We have the opportunity to build a Rainbow Bridge into the Golden Age. But to do this, we must do it together with all the colors of the rainbow, with all the peoples, all the beings of the world. We who are alive on Earth today are the Rainbow Warriors who face the challenge of building this bridge."

— Brooke Medicine Eagle Daughter of the Rainbow,
Crow, and Lakota medicine woman

The Rainbow Bridge

The concept of a bridge in time or a bridge to the future is extremely powerful. Since *The Rainbow Bridge* is deliberately global and includes and honors all people from all walks of life in all corners of the globe, it is by definition strong enough and wide enough for all people in the world to travel across. As we move forward together as world citizens, on any common community-building activities such as setting up brother and sister cities worldwide, planting trees, building bridges of understanding, envisioning the future we wish to create, helping to create the new global operating system, establishing an International Magna Carta or collaborating in many other ways to co-create a positive future, we need to do so in a coordinated, harmonious, and a unified fashion. It is for these reasons that the Rainbow Bridge is also a bridge from me to we and it is a bridge between many to One. It is a bridge to heart-based unity consciousness, Oneness, harmony and peace, both inner and outer.

"This would be a time when all the esoteric teachings of the world's traditions will be revealed, so there will be no secrets, no reason to fear each other, or to be in conflict. This is certainly what is happening now. Many are Rainbow Walkers…they are walking across The Rainbow Bridge to a new time."

— Oh Shinnah, medicine woman from Tineh (Apache), Mohawk, and Scottish origin

The Rainbow Bridge

"After the game is before the game."

— Sepp Herberger

New Beginnings

2012 marked a very important time for humankind. It marked the end of, ***and a new beginning*** of a 26,000 year cycle in the Mayan calendar. We have an incredible opportunity to consciously evolve to our next stage of evolution as a species, some say from our adolescent stage to our adulthood stage. In this light, we are in a time that is ripe for enormous expansion of consciousness, joy and abundance, both individually and collectively.

It is interesting to note that most of the world's major religions refer to an ending of time and a beginning of a new time, a new era. Bahá'í teachings refer to the coming Golden Age of international community; Buddhists refer to a time of darkness being followed by an auspicious time of joy, peace, and happiness; Christians refer to an apocalyptic end time followed by peace; Hindus refer to the ending of the Kali Yuga and beginning of the Satya Yuga or Golden Age of peace and prosperity; Jews refer to the "End of Days" followed by the Messianic Era; Muslims believe the new time will be marked by the "Day of Resurrection" followed by an era of peace; Native Americans and Indigenous peoples around the world speak of end times and a new time of peace and harmony with the

The Rainbow Bridge

Earth and all beings on it; and a fully developed concept of the end of time was also established in Zoroastrianism.

Is it possible that we are now in the prophesied time of an ending and a new beginning? Is it just an accident that the Mayan calendar accurately predicted the end of a major cycle followed by a new cycle, and that the major religious prophecies agree that there will be an ending of one era and a beginning of a new one?

The fact that we are faced with multiple simultaneous crises is actually an enormous opportunity, for if there was ever a time when we need to come together in a global, concerted, unified fashion, that time is now. While none of us know for sure what the future holds, it is imperative that we not create a self-fulfilling prophecy of doom and gloom. Regardless of the circumstances, it is important to approach our challenges by being cool, calm, collected, and rational. Regardless of whether you believe there is any validity to humanity experiencing an ending cycle and a new start cycle, we are being called to be conscious and to uphold a vision for the most inspiring and most positive future for all of humanity. We need each other to survive, and we need to put our heads and hearts together like we've never done before on a global basis, to collectively manifest a better life for all of humankind and for all of Earth's inhabitants.

Again, I am reminded of the thought that it is irresponsible to be pessimistic in a field of infinite possibilities. We can envision that the massive international collaborative effort to ensure there were no computer interruptions due to the Y2K computer bug (as we moved from 1999 to the year 2000) was a practice exercise. It prepared us to work together collectively as an international community to achieve a common goal — the positive and sustainable future of humanity. *The Rainbow Bridge* can help during any transition, during a "changing of the guard," in governments, corporations, or organizations of any kind. *The Rainbow Bridge* is a vehicle in consciousness and can serve as a bridge to the positive and exciting future that we all wish to experience.

As John Lennon said, "A dream you dream alone is only a dream. A dream you dream together is reality." There are millions of people around the world who know that the time for major change has arrived. Fortunately, millions of us are coming to the same conclusion and are coming together in a peaceful way to help bring about a new world that works for all.

There are a stunning number of people and organizations that are doing powerful work in their communities and in the world to help bring about a better world and "The Great Shift of the Ages," including, but definitely not limited to, the organizations listed elsewhere in this book and the following:

- American Sustainable Business Council
- Amnesty International
- Art of Living Foundation
- Association for Global New Thought
- Association of World Citizens
- Bill and Melinda Gates Foundation
- Bill, Hillary and Chelsea Clinton Foundation
- Bioneers
- BRAC
- Captain Planet Foundation

The Rainbow Bridge

- Center for Conscious Creativity (C3)
- Center for World Indigenous Studies
- Centre for Global Negotiations
- Cetacean Society International
- Children's Defense Fund
- Common Peace
- Council for a Parliament of World Religions
- Dan Millman's PeacefulWarrior.com
- Dream Change
- Dream University
- Earth Charter Initiative
- Earthdance
- Empower the UN
- Esalen Institute
- Foundation for Conscious Evolution
- Foundation for Mind Research
- Foundation for the Law of Time
- Gandhi Worldwide Education Institute
- Global Alliance for Transformational Entertainment (GATE)
- Global Commons Trust
- Global Movement for Children
- Globalisation for the Common Good
- Gordon and Betty Moore Foundation
- Grameen Foundation
- Greenpeace International
- Helen Caldicott Foundation for a Nuclear Free Planet
- Heritable Innovation Trust
- Humanity's Team
- Human Rights Action Center
- Human Rights Council
- Human Rights Watch
- Institute for Multi-Track Diplomacy
- Institute for Planetary Synthesis
- Institute for Sacred Activism
- Institute of Global Education
- Institute of Heartmath

The Rainbow Bridge

- Institute of Noetic Sciences
- Integral Institute
- International Day of Peace
- International Peace Bureau
- International Rescue Corps
- Intersections International
- Jane Goodall Institute
- Kosmos Journal
- Lindsay Wagner International
- Louis Gossett, Jr.'s Eracism Foundation
- Martin Luther King Foundation
- Musk Foundation
- National Peace Academy
- Nelson Mandela Foundation
- Nobel Women's Initiative
- Not On Our Watch
- Nuclear Age Peace Foundation
- Nuclear Threat Initiative (NTI)
- Office of the U.N. High Commissioner for Human Rights
- Omega Institute
- On The Commons
- ONE
- Open Society Foundations
- P2P Foundation
- Pathways to Peace
- Paul G. Allen Family Foundation
- PeaceJam
- PeaceLink
- Peace One Day
- Peace People
- People's Movement for Human Rights Learning
- Search for Common Ground
- Share the World's Resources
- Shari Arison's businesses and foundations
- Sir Richard Branson's Virgin Unite
- Skoll Foundation

The Rainbow Bridge

- Stanford Peace Innovation Lab
- Student Peace Alliance
- Synergy Foundation
- TED (Technology, Entertainment, Design)
- Temple Hayes Ministries
- The Atlantic Philanthropies
- The Carter Center
- The Center for Non-Violent Communication
- The Charter for Compassion
- The Chopra Foundation
- The Climate Reality Project
- The Club of Budapest
- The Dalai Lama Foundation
- The Desmond Tutu Peace Foundation
- The Disclosure Project
- The Elders
- The Global Citizens' Initiative (TGCI)
- The Gorbachev Foundation
- The Hunger Project
- The Oprah Winfrey Foundation
- The Pachamama Alliance
- The Peace Alliance
- The Richardson Center for Global Engagement
- The Twilight Brigade
- Thrive
- Transformational Leadership Council
- Turner Endangered Species Fund
- Turner Foundation
- U.N. Educational, Scientific and Cultural Organization (UNESCO)
- United Nations
- United Nations Association of the USA
- United Nations Foundation
- United Religions Initiative
- Virgin Unite
- Water.org

The Rainbow Bridge

- Whitaker Peace & Development Initiative
- World Business Academy
- World Citizen Foundation
- World Commission on Global Consciousness and Spirituality
- World Federation of United Nations Associations
- World Future Society
- World Nature Organization (WNO)
- World Wide Fund For Nature (WWF)
- Worldwatch Institute
- Youth and Elders Project
- Yunus Centre

…and many, many more.

We are in a time of unprecedented opportunity. This is a time when each of us is being called to examine our priorities, to look at our lives and at our beliefs. Collectively, the opportunity we have as a species and a single family of human beings is nothing less than choosing the survival of our species and all life on the planet. Will we be driven by our fear, insecurities, and multiple global challenges that may appear to be irresolvable…believing that the future is out of our control? Or will we collectively decide that it is up to us to harness the power of our intention, the power of our faith, the power we have to choose to believe in a positive future, and our overall willpower to consciously choose a positive and sustainable future? I believe we will choose to create a positive future that works for everyone. The inclusive language of the universal principles plays a major role in creating a global framework and common ground in which we can live and work together with one another in peace, harmony, and abundance.

The Rainbow Bridge

"Unconditional war can no longer lead to unconditional victory. It can no longer serve to settle disputes. It can no longer be of concern to great powers alone. For a nuclear disaster, spread by winds and waters and fear, could well engulf the great and the small, the rich and the poor, the committed and the uncommitted alike. Mankind must put an end to war or war will put an end to mankind."

— U.S. President John F. Kennedy

Eliminating Nuclear Weapons

The existence of nuclear weapons poses a grave threat to the safety and survival of all humanity and indeed, all life on the planet. As long as there are nuclear weapons in the world, it is possible that they will be used, intentionally or accidentally. In addition, as long as nuclear weapons exist, it will be possible for nuclear materials to be lost, stolen, or illegally sold. In a world where billions of people live in poverty, the risk of nuclear weapons or nuclear materials falling into the wrong hands is a frightening possibility.

According to the Nuclear Age Peace Foundation, in 1986 there were more than 70,000 nuclear weapons in the world, most of which were located in the U.S. and U.S.S.R.. Since the mid-1980s, the world has eliminated roughly 53,000 of these horrific devices, leaving about 17,000 nuclear weapons in the world today. Although we have made impressive progress, we still have a great deal of work to do in order to eliminate this dangerous threat to civilization.

Rather than using precious financial resources, brain power, time, and energy to build bigger and more powerful nuclear weapons of mass destruction, it is far more responsible to focus on identifying and resolving the root causes of the issues that face us. To ensure the elimination of the horrors of nuclear weapons, we must continue to strive to educate and mobilize the global public in countless ways.

Until nuclear weapons are made illegal and until all of them are eliminated, the world will needlessly be a more dangerous place for everyone.

"Nuclear weapons are monstrous and obscene. Nuclear war would destroy civilization and place the human species at risk of annihilation. The threat or use of nuclear weapons is immoral and would constitute a war crime and a crime against humanity. Zero is the only safe number of nuclear weapons on the planet. Committed and concerted leadership and action to achieve Nuclear Zero is long overdue."

— Dr. David Krieger, Founder and President of the Nuclear Age Peace Foundation (www.wagingpeace.org), and author and editor of many books, including *Hope in a Dark Time* and *ZERO: The Case for Nuclear Weapons Abolition*

The Rainbow Bridge

"A native elder tells her granddaughter that we each have two wolves that are fighting inside of ourselves. One wolf is mean and the other is gentle. The granddaughter asks the elder, 'Grandmother, which one wins?' The wise grandmother answers, 'Which ever one we feed the most.'"

— Native Wisdom Teaching

Eliminating Terrorism

The challenge of terrorism is a direct result of people feeling desperate and angry; religious conflicts are side effects, not root causes. Poverty and lack of hope are root causes of terrorism. To solve our global problems, including terrorism, we must address the root causes. The unfair and inequitable distribution of resources is the root cause of many global issues. This problem will be addressed as we embark on a journey to create a smoothly functioning global operating system intelligently and transparently designed for and by The People. Those who would commit acts of terrorism in the past will no longer be so disenfranchised and desperate, and the side effects of terrorism caused by widespread poverty will gradually fade away. We can be inspired knowing that the solution is simple — although not necessarily easy. Let the simplicity of the solution be a guiding light, and as the quote on the top of this page suggests, let us choose to feed the gentle wolf with our time, energy, resources, and love.

The Rainbow Bridge

"The pendulum of the mind alternates between sense and nonsense, not between right and wrong."

— Dr. Carl Jung

Is the Earth Round or Flat?

Even after it became widely known that the earth is not flat, many people refused to change their beliefs. It took hundreds of years for this fact to become accepted as consensus reality. It is shocking that there are still people today who believe the earth is flat! All one needs to do is search the Internet for "Flat Earth Society" to find thousands of people who still share this erroneous belief. Despite the solid evidence, and billions with the shared view of a round earth, they believe the earth is flat. They might wonder, "How could we be incorrect when so many other people agree with us?" Yet it is clear that the belief the earth is flat is simply inaccurate, based on scientific facts.

Just because other people agree with you, doesn't mean you are "on the right side of history." When our beliefs are aligned with the available facts, we can make incredible progress, as individuals in our personal lives and collectively as a world community. When we are dealing with issues of life and death and the future of our planet, this point is extremely important to remember.

The Rainbow Bridge

As we become global-thinking world citizens, aware of and utilizing concepts such as universal principles, we can recognize that global problems require global solutions. As we begin to think about the need to have a smoothly functioning, global operating system, the question regarding the accuracy of our thoughts and beliefs is indeed an important one to consider. Just because there might be naysayers and people who don't yet fully comprehend the path to resolve our global challenges, doesn't mean they are accurate in their beliefs.

Do you feel we have everything we need to create a smoothly functioning, harmonious, and abundant world community? Or do you have a hard time seeing the world as a peaceful, abundant place where the needs of all people are met? Are there any areas of your life where you might be thinking in a flat Earth way?

I believe we can create a better world. Sometimes, when navigating through the rough waters of life, we need to "put our thinking caps on" and to "keep our wits about us" as we resolve to solve our challenges peacefully through informed conversation, dialogue, and diplomacy — formally, informally, one-on-one, and in groups.

"Intelligence is the ability to adapt to change."

— Dr. Stephen Hawking

The Rainbow Bridge

"Courage is what it takes to stand up and speak;
courage is also what it takes to sit down and listen."

— Prime Minister of the UK, Winston Churchill

Global Dialogues

Progress between individuals and organizations comes about through purposeful conversation and dialogue. Even though this may seem obvious, it is a critical concept to how we will resolve the myriad challenges we face. Conversation, dialogue and diplomacy at the global level, including people and organizations from all walks of life, are of paramount importance in creating a world that works for all.

This subject is so important that we have already started developing plans for an initiative to facilitate these conversations and dialogues. This project as we envision it is called "The Global Dialogues," and a brief summary follows:

Vision

The Global Dialogues project envisions the peoples of the world engaged in a series of purposeful conversations and dialogues, leading toward the development of a smoothly functioning global operating system. We envision people from all professions, age groups, religions, nations, and all corners of the world talking about matters of concern to humanity at this historic time. We envision people enthusiastically participating in informed intentional dialogue both online, as well as offline in the "real world." We envision The Global Dialogues helping to bridge the gap between what is reported in the media and what is happening in the "real world." Our intention is to help create a more equitable and sustainable future for the World Community. We are guided by the principles in The Earth Charter, a worldwide campaign launched in March of 2000 after eight years of discussion involving more than 100,000 people in 51 countries.

Mission

The mission of The Global Dialogues project is to stimulate and facilitate a large-scale series of informed conversations and dialogues worldwide, both online and in the "real world," for the purpose of helping to create a better world for everyone.

Fact-Based Information Center

Facts are important. We will ensure that conversation, dialogue, and diplomacy are informed by facts to the greatest extent possible. Our fact-based Information Center will ensure that questions are researched and answers are uncovered based on concrete facts.

The Network Model:
Collaboration, Cooperation, and Non-Competition

Thanks to the hard work, dedication and commitment of numerous individuals and organizations, various types of meaningful communication and dialogues are taking place all over the world. The Global Dialogues does not aim to reinvent the wheel or be in competition with any existing organizations; to the extent that we can collaborate, cooperate and recognize that we are not in competition with one another, all of our efforts toward making a

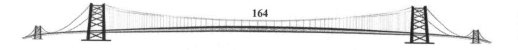

better world will be more effective and fruitful. The Global Dialogues can also be viewed as facilitating the creation of a global network of networks. Quality online and offline conversations, already taking place, are warmly welcomed into The Global Dialogues, as are organizations and projects that provide "conversation starter" information and material. One of our goals is to link together all of the existing dialogue and conversation projects currently underway, increasing the visibility and exposure for everyone along the way.

Dialogues that Can Lead to Group Action

Our plans include the use of easy-to-use online polls and surveys to analyze input on critical issues and topics of discussion. Participants who wish to join action oriented groups to address specific issues will be assisted by state-of-the-art information and communication systems to facilitate sharing of information, communication, collaboration, and networking. In the spirit of evolution and not revolution, together we can make a difference and leave the planet better than we found it.

The Rainbow Bridge

*"The dream of a world united against the awful wastes of war is...
deeply embedded in the heart of humanity...and there must be,
not just a balance of power, but a community of power;
not organized rivalries but an organized common peace."*

— U.S. President Woodrow Wilson

The Rainbow Bridge Road Map to World Peace

This section summarizes some of the most important actions we can take to help create a bridge to a better world. It is a framework and road map that leads to an organized common peace in our quest to help design and build a smoothly functioning, global operating system.

Fundamental Tenets

- Take collective action — both locally and globally — to help design and engineer a smoothly functioning global operating system for the purpose of creating a better world where the basic needs of everyone are met.
- Leverage and upgrade existing systems, organizations, and institutions wherever feasible.
- Operate using the ethos "unity amidst diversity," appreciating and celebrating our myriad differences while operating in a unified, harmonious fashion.
- Resist the temptation of short-term thinking; we must design a system that is sustainable, long-lasting, and able to adapt to future needs.

The Rainbow Bridge

- Utilize calm, level-headed, logical conversation, dialogue, and diplomacy in everything we do.
- Utilize universal principles in every aspect of our plans and actions.
- Contribute to community development on a global basis.
- Avoid the common practice of obtaining an answer to every question before we get started.

"Nothing will ever be attempted
if all possible objections must first be overcome."

— Samuel Johnson

Summary of The Rainbow Bridge Road Map to World Peace

1. Create a world-class team consisting of doctors, lawyers, astronauts, Olympians, Ambassadors, Nobel Laureates, global-thinking luminaries, philanthropists, celebrities, leading universities, and thoughtful, everyday people whose mission is to recommend ways to plan and take collective action towards creating a smoothly functioning, global operating system. The Rainbow Bridge Road Map to World Peace serves as the framework for discussion and collective action.

2. Modernize and restructure the United Nations:
   a. Restructure the U.N. Security Council to ensure fair and balanced representation from all U.N. member states.
   b. Restructure the Security Council so it is subordinated to the General Assembly.
   c. In addition to the U.N. General Assembly, create a way to directly incorporate the voice of The People, such as a U.N. People's Assembly.

The Rainbow Bridge

    d.   Work with the U.N. Change Management Team (CMT) to identify and implement other desirable changes.

3.   Empower, support, and promote efforts designed to create a unified Global Commons Plan/Global Marshall Plan and a commons-based economy.

4.   Explore ways to create a carefully-planned global Jubilee, in conjunction with the implementation of a commons-based economy, to eliminate debt and ensure a fair and equitable way to start a "new game" and a new era of peace and harmony worldwide.

5.   Promote the movement of Departments and Ministries of Peace in nations around the world. Wherever there is a Department or Ministry of Defense, there should also be a Department or Ministry of Peace reporting at the same level, to ensure a balanced approach to securing peace and security.

6.   Promote the Gross National Happiness (GNH) concept and Happiness Index, to ensure that we always understand how happy we really are. It is difficult to improve what we do not measure, so it makes sense that we would take steps to measure the overall happiness and well-being of The People around the world.

7.   Spearhead the development of an Inner Health Program. Everyone in the world wants to be happy and to live a life free of stress and pressure. Since peace always starts within our own individual hearts and minds, a comprehensive road map for peace would not be complete without a focus on inner peace.

8.   Promote initiatives and organizations whose critical mission is to eliminate nuclear weapons from the planet. Committed,

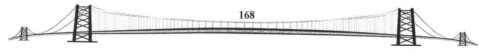

unified and sustained leadership and action are of utmost importance not only to all of humanity, but also to all life forms on our planet.

9. Modernize and upgrade the way we conduct business:
   a. All businesses should operate in a socially responsible manner and receive certification, which includes being open ("open source") and transparent. This includes socially responsible treatment of:
      i. Employees and third-party contractors, vendors, and partners (including initiatives to identify and eliminate workplace bullying)
      ii. Customers
      iii. Communities in which business is conducted

   b. Promote hybrid business models. One brilliant and inspiring example is Blue Shield of California, a not-for-profit mutual benefit corporation and health plan with no shareholders. They pledge to limit their annual net income and if they exceed this amount, they return the difference to their customers and to the community.[2]

   c. As long as central banks exist, ensure that they operate in a fully transparent manner, including, but not limited to, ensuring the clear identity of all shareholders and their respective percent of ownership.

10. Promote initiatives and organizations that continue the critical task of protecting our precious environment and addressing the global climate crisis.

---

[2] Blue Shield of California pledges to limit their annual net income to 2% of revenue and if they earn more than 2%, they return the difference to their customers and to the community. As of December 2012, they have returned an astonishing $470 million back to the community!

The Rainbow Bridge

11. Promote initiatives and organizations helping to research and produce clean, renewable forms of energy.

12. Launch an international project to create an International Magna Carta for the 21st century and beyond.

13. Kick off The Global Dialogues, with a Fact-Based Information Center, via the Earth Communications Center or similar socially-responsible, dedicated, international communications infrastructure and social network.

14. Initiate a World Citizenship Program with a strong educational component, potentially shepherded by the United Nations University for Peace in Costa Rica.

The above road map is a starting point that will involve extensive conversation, dialogue and diplomacy regarding priorities, sequencing, costs, and details. There will be detractors and cynics, but let this not stop us from coming together in unity amidst our diversity to create a bridge to a harmonious and sustainable future. Just like creating or debugging a large and complex computer system, when we break down the challenges and take one step at a time, we can indeed be successful. As Voltaire observed, "No problem can withstand the assault of sustained thinking."

Finally, let us not insist that every question be answered before we get started, and let us build the bridge before the river swells.

"A good plan today is better than a perfect plan tomorrow."

— From the movie *Wag the Dog*

The Rainbow Bridge

"These Two Leggeds will be called the Rainbow Tribe, for they are the product of thousands of years of melding among the five original races. These Children of Earth have been called together to open their hearts and to move beyond the barriers of disconnection. The medicine they carry is the Whirling Rainbow of Peace, which will mark the union of the five races as one."

— From *Other Council Fires Were Here Before Ours*
by Jamie Sams

Implications

If the universal principles in this book are followed diligently and with deep commitment, they will help lead us toward inner and outer peace, happiness, and joy. It is important that each of us do what we can to manifest inner peace in our own lives, for we impact the lives of everyone whether we come in contact with them or not. In addition, just as the universal principles can be applied to our individual lives, they can also be applied in every other area of our lives, as individuals and collectively in our institutions.

To be sure, our world is in crisis. To some extent, it always has been. The difference at this juncture in our evolution is that we have the ability to make an extraordinary breakthrough and transformation toward implementing universal principles in all fields of endeavor, including but not limited to business, politics, economics, the media, government, legal system, science, health, medicine, culture, spirituality, art, music, ecology, etc. — *on a global scale.* With the advances made in science and technology, we are able to reach literally billions of people in the blink of an eye

The Rainbow Bridge

with a message of commonality, peace, and humanity — all based on the shared principles enumerated in *The Rainbow Bridge*. All we need to do is ask ourselves a few simple questions:

- Are we conscientiously applying universal principles in all areas of our lives as individuals?

- Are we consciously building bridges of understanding between people, religions, races, cultures, businesses, organizations, and nations?

- Do our governmental institutions utilize universal principles?

- Does our world of business and commerce operate according to universal principles?

- Do our media organizations implement universal principles?

- Do our financial, educational, scientific, and legal institutions consciously utilize universal principles?

- Are we individually or collectively doing unto others what we would not want done to ourselves?

Your answer to these questions may be "no." But, if you're reading this book, then one fact is obvious: you want to do something to make a change. Within you is a yearning, even if it's a small glimmer, for a better world, one in which the traits of integrity, responsibility, authenticity, accountability, respect, honesty, compassion, and love are the core of daily life. All it takes is one step, an individual step, to help bring about that world we are all seeking. And it is important to remember that each step we take, no matter how small or large, contributes toward uplifting all of humanity. That's how important each of us is — we are an integral light in the vast shining light of consciousness. Individually, we are magnificent. Collectively, we are truly unlimited.

Imagine what life would be like if more people understood and lived by "as you think, so it is…karma is cause and effect…balance and moderation…surrender…acting 'as if'…the power of thought… discernment…and live and let live." Just sit for a moment and envision how different the world would be. How would people treat each other? What if we didn't judge each other but instead saw each of us as a radiant spark of light? What if each of us let go of our fears knowing that change is actually for our own good because there is always more to learn, to investigate and to discover about ourselves, about humanity, about life?

The implications are astounding and within our grasp. As I stated earlier, the principles in this book are simple and simply expressed, though not necessarily easily brought about. The beauty of each of the universal principles is that they *are* simple. Nothing complicated, austere, intellectually challenging — just elegantly and unpretentiously straightforward. And each can be applied in your personal life, with your family, at work, and in your community. All it takes is one step and building on that step day by day.

The Rainbow Bridge

Life is a mystery. But it's less of a mystery if we choose to explore beyond the boundaries of what we know, of what we see in front of us, of what we experience with just our five senses. It's all a matter of what we choose to focus on. Where are your thoughts centered most of the time? Imagine what could happen if we explored beyond our rational self — keeping in mind the universal principles — and applied what we discovered to business, science, our systems of governance, our economic/financial/banking systems, our media, and our culture.

Our Personal Lives

As mentioned throughout this book, the world we live in is a collective manifestation of our inner worlds and belief systems on a global basis. In addition to using universal principles in our quiet moments, we can use them to learn more about ourselves, to understand what is important to ourselves, and to help navigate the challenges of life. We can also use them in every thought we have and in every action we take, including with our family, friends, colleagues, and acquaintances. As we incorporate the use of universal principles, we can understand that we are actually upgrading our own internal operating systems, continually removing issues and becoming more finely tuned, efficient and effective, not to mention smoothly functioning. Once we make it a habit, universal principles can be utilized to our mutual benefit in every other aspect of our lives, as individuals and collectively as a world community.

Business

More and more people worldwide are recognizing and discussing the fact that there are numerous unregulated corporations focused *only* on the single bottom line of "financial success," that are inadvertently helping to bring about starvation, poverty, and tremendous suffering throughout the world. As a result, the business world is fraught with troubles. One example is the corporate scandals currently plaguing America brought about by extraordinary greed, a lack of respect for people, and a complete disregard of universal principles. The negative effect on billions of lives is astounding.

> *"Capital as such is not evil; it is its wrong use that is evil.*
> *Capital in some form or other will always be needed."*

> — Mahatma Gandhi

However, what is very exciting to see is that a new heart-centered corporate ethos is emerging from this crisis. It is based on social responsibility and conscious capitalism, a movement toward businesses operating not on just a *single bottom line* of financial success, but on a *triple bottom line:* financial success for all parties involved, environmental protection, and social equity. The global advent of B Corporations and Benefit Corporations, which have mandates to perform in a socially responsible manner, are excellent steps in the right direction. Businesses that wish to align themselves in a socially responsible manner and to serve the common good now have increased resources such as ISO 26000, created by the

The Rainbow Bridge

International Standards Organization. ISO 26000 provides guidance for all types of organizations, regardless of their size or location, on:

1. Concepts, terms, and definitions related to social responsibility.
2. Background, trends, and characteristics of social responsibility.
3. Principles and practices relating to social responsibility.
4. Core subjects and issues of social responsibility.
5. Integrating, implementing, and promoting socially responsible behavior throughout the organization and, through its policies and practices, within its sphere of influence.
6. Identifying and engaging with all stakeholders.
7. Communicating commitments, performance, and other information related to social responsibility.

Furthermore, there are a growing number of investment funds that will only invest in companies adhering to principles of conscious capitalism and social responsibility. All of these developments are very exciting indeed.

"Ethical and responsible behavior needs to become the cornerstone of corporate behavior."

— Dr. Manmohan Singh, Prime Minister of India

The Rainbow Bridge

Businesses of the future can become fully sustainable and actually flourish economically in the long run if universal principles continue to be incorporated and utilized both on an individual basis with each employee and as an organization within the larger context of global business.

Economic/Financial/Banking Systems

Arguably, the existing global economic, financial, and banking systems have allowed humanity to survive up to this point in time. However, it is clear that the current global financial system is going through a serious crisis and needs to be changed. One of the reasons goes back to the lack of a smoothly functioning, global operating system. The fact that we have currencies and businesses that compete rather than collaborate with one another is a direct result of having an "us-them" mentality. Once we understand that the world is a completely interconnected and interdependent system, and that we are truly members of one family of people on this planet, we can create a transparent global economic system that is holistic in nature...a system that is sustainable and that serves the common good globally, as opposed to the other way around.

"If Congress has the right under the Constitution to issue paper money, it was given to be used by themselves, not to be delegated to individuals or corporations."

— U.S. President Andrew Jackson

The Rainbow Bridge

Banks should be more than regular businesses. At their core, they should be guardians of The People's assets. Banks should be socially responsible instruments that serve the needs of The People; entities that serve the public good. Instead, entities such as central banks are frequently not owned by The People, but often by anonymous private individuals and entities. Although anonymity and lack of transparency might make sense to some bankers, transparency is clearly a more optimal design given the number of people and life forms at stake. This is especially true when a central bank controls the issuance of a nation's currency. Therefore, the current non-transparent central banking model is outdated and should be upgraded along with the rest of the 21st century global operating system. The development of a commons-based economy will likely play a pivotal role in this much-needed upgrade.

Governance

There has perhaps never been a more important time in history to incorporate the use of universal principles in all forms of governance around the world. Without the conscious use of universal principles, the military-industrial complex that U.S. President Dwight D. Eisenhower so astutely warned us about will wittingly or unwittingly continue to exert unwarranted influence. As a reminder of the tremendous wisdom imparted by a sitting U.S. President and a highly respected, highly decorated, 5-star general, here is part of his farewell address:

> *"...In the councils of government, we must guard against the acquisition of unwarranted influence,*

whether sought or unsought, by the military industrial complex. The potential for the disastrous rise of misplaced power exists and will persist.

We must never let the weight of this combination endanger our liberties or democratic processes. We should take nothing for granted. Only an alert and knowledgeable citizenry can compel the proper meshing of the huge industrial and military machinery of defense with our peaceful methods and goals, so that security and liberty may prosper together...."

For an important, shocking and eye-opening account of what can happen through misplaced power and gross lack of universal principles, please refer to the N.Y. Times bestseller *Confessions of an Economic Hit Man* by John Perkins. Much like reading *The Art of War* by Sun Tzu, this book is disturbing and yet useful in understanding the financial warfare happening behind the scenes in America and around the world. It is also inspiring because the book shows how we can make changes to help bring about a better world for all.

Media

We have some of the world's most sophisticated tools and concepts at hand to disseminate information from television to computers and the Internet to movies, radio, books, newspapers, and magazines. Much of what is focused on, though, highlights the ills of our society and communities around the world. People seem to have a

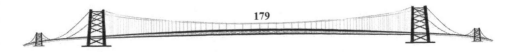

The Rainbow Bridge

penchant for gravitating toward the sensational and destructive rather than toward substance and what uplifts.

Knowing this, media producers give the public what they seem to clamor for consistently. Yet the impact of media on people both young and old is tremendous, especially for impressionable young minds that don't have a perspective about what they are taking in. It is amazing to think, though, that when we are young, our view of the world is so different: fresh, awe inspired, inviting, exciting, and simple. Along the way, we lose sight of that initial perspective. We forget that life is a dream, about following our hearts, respecting our elders, and that we can step through the looking glass.

What the media and entertainment industry reports on or presents to the public has the ability to influence and create shifts in the perceptions and beliefs of its readers and viewers. What messages are we trying to put across? Are we trying to inspire, uplift, inform, and expand? Or are we just trying to make the greatest amount of money possible by whatever means no matter what the cost to the public and environment?

We owe it to ourselves and our children, to create a new system, one that centers not on the bottom line, but the essential messages grounded in universal principles supporting the highest good for all concerned. Fortunately, media is being redefined in cyberspace… social media is the media of the 21st century.

Science

There are two main paradigms limiting us: (1) we ignore what we cannot see and measure, and (2) we predict future events by relying solely on evidence gained from past events and interpretations. In context, both are appropriate and applicable. Yet there are times when scientific theory can't explain the phenomena of our lives: manifestation through intention, governing our bodies through thoughtful focus, spontaneous healing and self-healing, telekinesis, remote viewing and remote influencing, out of body and near-death experiences, etc. The power of thought and willpower are simply not taken into consideration and must be in order for science to be complete.

Scientists could make even more extraordinary advancements if they applied universal principles in their work. Simply by recognizing that even just the act of observing something changes an outcome and our perspective is something to be reckoned with, not ignored because it isn't measurable by scientific standards. Our thoughts — imagination, creative musings, daydreams, visualizations — are the seeds of physical manifestation, as witnessed by the multitude of accomplishments surrounding us, whether personal or public.

Immeasurable by science, but fact nonetheless — we are interconnected in a vast matrix of can't-be-measured consciousness. Science must deal with this, even if we only admit that we are not using all of the data available to us. This in and of itself would be a major accomplishment because it would bring this issue to full consciousness.

Culture

We live in one of the most sophisticated cultures ever developed. The technology, arts, commerce, law, governance, and other institutions we've created are extraordinary. Yet we still suffer from race issues, poverty, violence, inequality, and ignorance. And we still feel the need to use the threat of violence and war as a means to "create peace." We spend an enormous amount of time, energy, and money on perfecting the instruments of war and protecting what we consider ours, even to the detriment of other peoples and cultures. The matrix of big profits, the push for more resources, global positioning, and materially-based lifestyles have blinded us to a clearer focus — the focus of our commonalities, of sharing and being of service without thought of return, that what we give we shall receive, of taking responsibility and gaining a larger perspective.

We must have an open and earnest dialogue to determine in just what direction we'd like to progress, not in terms of unbridled advancement without thought to the future, but how to go about helping facilitate the creation of a global, wisdom-based culture of peace. It is a major undertaking, but it is completely within our capability as spiritual beings having a human experience.

Each of the areas above will be covered in greater depth in future volumes that will include concrete examples and practical methods for applying the principles described in *The Rainbow Bridge*. It is important to recognize that *it is in our own best interest* to take in and apply these principles, not only on an individual basis, but in all areas of our lives and to share them with others. Examples abound of what can happen when we ignore or set aside these principles. Just look at the strife, unhappiness, conflict, anger, and turmoil in our world today. Do we continue along this path and possibly annihilate ourselves in the process? Or do we stop, observe ourselves and the outcomes of our endeavors, and *take action* to create a better world based upon these universal principles?

The Rainbow Bridge is about helping us to choose and to create a better way. In the past, the universal principles listed here have never been put forth in a fashion that was easily accessible or even collected in one book. I have attempted to articulate these principles in a clear and concise manner so as to remove the shrouds of secrecy, ambiguity, or complexity that have for so long kept us from becoming greater versions of ourselves. As I stated earlier, these principles are simple yet may not be easily lived. However, the more we practice living them day by day, the more we will discover just how intrinsic they are to our Being.

PART FIVE

The Way Forward

"The mystery of human existence lies not in just staying alive, but in finding something to live for."

— Fyodor Dostoyevsky

The Rainbow Bridge

*"If you are not fulfilled, it may be because
you are not pursuing your destiny."*

— Anthony Chisom

What is Your Life Purpose?

Do you understand why you are here at his critical time in history? What your purpose in life is? What legacy do you wish to leave to the world when you are no longer here? What your destiny is?

These are important questions to reflect upon, not only because it will help you move toward greater inner peace and tranquility, but also since it will help you utilize your talents, abilities, and passion to help make a positive difference in the world.

One of the universal principles is being of service to someone else or to a cause that is larger than our own individual selves. The satisfaction we gain when we are contributing to others in the spirit of service can be very profound. Often, when we choose to be of service to others, our own challenges can pale in comparison, which can allow us to shift our focus and change how we feel about our own issues. We can clearly see that our lives really do make a difference, and this can be profoundly gratifying.

When pondering the question about the purpose of our lives, could it possibly be that it is to be of service to humanity? I believe on some

The Rainbow Bridge

level all of us feel a deep calling to be of service to humanity and that we just might not know what to do. If you have resonated with this book and the concept of building a bridge to our collective future, perhaps you would like to lend some of your unique energy and talents to the growing of this movement towards inner peace and world peace. Talk about *The Rainbow Bridge* and universal principles with your friends and family, and know that it is real; it already exists.

The Rainbow Bridge

"If the success or failure of this planet and of human beings
depended on how I am and what I do, how would I be?
What would I do?"

— Buckminster Fuller

A Call to Action

If you feel a call to find your own inner peace and to help facilitate world peace using the universal principles of *The Rainbow Bridge*, please share it with your friends, family, colleagues, social networks, newspapers, and television stations and give it away as a gift. This is extremely important — how can we all be on the same page as a global family if we're not reading the same book?

"Rome is burning, son! The problem is with us,
all of us who do nothing, who just fiddle...
who try to maneuver around the edges of the flame."

— From the movie *Lions for Lambs*

In addition, you will find benefit in reading this book at least a few times, as each time you will see and understand things differently. Listen to the audiobook on your computer, on your mobile device or on CD. Go to www.TheRainbowBridge.org to engage in conversation and dialogue, and to network and collaborate with many other people. Pick at least one meditation, or create your own, and practice it daily for at least 20 minutes or as much as you can (you can start at 5 minutes and work your way up to 20 or more minutes if you desire).

We are being called to deliberate action right now. We have a responsibility to leave the world a better place than we found it. If you feel a call to be "on The Rainbow Bridge", "on The People's Bridge" or "on Humanity's Bridge," perhaps assisting with building the Rainbow Bridge worldwide, please visit us at www.TheRainbowBridge.org and feel free to send us a message at Support@TheRainbowBridge.org .

"You must be the change you wish to see in the world."

— Mahatma Gandhi

Philanthropic Program

We want as many people as possible to have access to *The Rainbow Bridge* regardless of their financial means. Our initial goal is to give away 5 million copies of *The Rainbow Bridge* through the generous support of like-minded people, organizations, and businesses. Mass copies of *The Rainbow Bridge* can be purchased for as little as 10% above cost through this special philanthropic initiative. Special acknowledgement of the donor on the inside of the books is also possible.

If you want to be part of the team facilitating the distribution of complimentary copies of *The Rainbow Bridge* in schools, libraries,

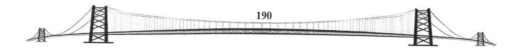

community centers, orphanages, child care centers, foster care homes, homeless shelters, hospices, retirement homes, meditation centers, community mental health centers, juvenile detention centers, rehabilitation centers and prisons, please send us a message at Distribution@TheRainbowBridge.org .

In order to help people learn about universal principles in a fun, entertaining and yet educational manner, we have created and piloted The Rainbow Bridge Game of Life board game, which will be available for distribution in the near future. Please stay tuned to our website for further updates.

The Rainbow Bridge Road Map to World Peace

If your interest was piqued by something you read in this book, such as being involved in the implementation of the Road Map to World Peace, including helping to create the new global operating system, the creation of an International Magna Carta, setting up brother and sister cities worldwide, planting trees, helping with transportation, bridge and road-building projects, educational projects, housing and community center projects, food, water, clean energy, and environmental projects or anything else, please visit our main website, as well as the Earth Communications Center, which is currently in development.

Join the movement for peace by connecting with The Rainbow Bridge on multiple social networks to spread goodwill:

Main website: www.TheRainbowBridge.org

The Rainbow Bridge

Come join the global network for harmony, reconciliation and unity, and for the conscious evolution of humanity!

"There is one thing stronger than all the armies in the world, and that is, an idea whose time has come."

— Victor Hugo

PART SIX

Additional Information

Prophecy of The Rainbow Bridge

During a time of great darkness, the Earth's waters will be dirty, the air polluted, the land ravaged and filled with warring peoples. During this time of unrest and sadness, a great new wind will blow across the land worldwide.

People of all colors will come together in the spirit of love, compassion, peace, unity, reconciliation, and understanding with respect for the sanctity of all life, the sanctity of nature, and the sanctity of the Earth herself.

These humble and courageous people in all corners of the world will be known by many names: Rainbow Warriors, Light Warriors, Rainbow Children of God, Light Workers, Rainbow Tribe, and Peaceful Warriors. They will come together and resolve their mutual problems as adults with the recognition that they are guardians of a positive future and are caretakers of the Earth for all future generations.

These people of many colors will share their universal truths with one another from their hearts, and they will see that their truths are all the same, but with different names and forms. The medicine they carry is the Whirling Rainbow of Peace, it will connect their heads and their hearts, and it will connect them to one another. These multi-colored people will come together in the spirit of unity amidst their diversity; they will spread a wave of love, compassion,

The Rainbow Bridge

wisdom, peace and harmony; they will help restore balance in all areas of life; and they will help change the face of the world forever.

By coming together as one family while following their common truths, they will walk across a bridge in time together — The Rainbow Bridge to Peace.

The Rainbow Bridge

*"You never change things by fighting the existing reality.
To change something, build a new model
that makes the old model obsolete."*

— Buckminster Fuller

Summary of The Rainbow Bridge Vision

- *The Rainbow Bridge* book illuminates the common ground in all religions and receives distribution worldwide. It is translated into numerous languages and formats.

- The Rainbow Bridge Initiative continues with a series of books, systematically applying the universal principles found in *The Rainbow Bridge* in a variety of fields in concrete and practical ways.

- To help our sisters and brothers in need, a large number of corporate, organizational and individual sponsors purchase copies of *The Rainbow Bridge* for free distribution in schools, libraries, orphanages, child care centers, foster care homes, homeless shelters, hospices, retirement homes, meditation centers, community mental health centers, juvenile detention centers, rehabilitation centers, and prisons.

The Rainbow Bridge

- A rainbow-colored tribe of people from all walks of life from all corners of the world comes together in the spirit of creating more cooperation, harmony, understanding, reconciliation, happiness, unity, and abundance worldwide.

- A grassroots global phenomenon is created. A massive "network of networks" mobilizes to take part in conversations and dialogues that lead to greater understanding and appreciation of each other worldwide.

- *The Rainbow Bridge* helps accelerate the transformation of business and commerce using heart-centered, socially responsible business practices.

- A large, online presence is created to facilitate communication, dialogues and greater understanding of other peoples, cultures, and ways of life worldwide. It is literally a portal to a new world.

- A fun and entertaining board game is distributed that allows people all over the world to explore universal principles.

- An interactive television series is broadcast in major cities worldwide.

The Rainbow Bridge

- A major mainstream movie sweeps the planet, spreading a wave of goodwill, inspiration, and excitement.

- Additional physical Rainbow Bridges and Rainbow Bridge stores are built around the world, especially in conjunction with international friendship-oriented brother and sister city programs.

- People come together to be involved in helping implement The Rainbow Bridge Road Map to World Peace, to help plan and create a new global operating system, to help create an International Magna Carta, to set up brother and sister cities worldwide, to create the new global operating system, to plant trees, to facilitate transportation, bridge and road-building projects, educational projects, housing and community center projects, as well as food, water and clean energy projects, celebrations, and more.

- The Rainbow Bridge Road Map to World Peace using universal principles is implemented, which helps to transform our current global economic system based on competition to a global economic system based on collaboration, partnership, and harmony.

The Rainbow Bridge

- The Rainbow Bridge Road Map to World Peace helps to bridge the gap between our old systems that are slowly disintegrating to a new system that works for all people everywhere.

- To the astonishment of many people, the world enters an unprecedented era of peace, harmony, unity, and abundance.

Acknowledgments

Writing a book requires the support and assistance of numerous people. My deepest heartfelt thanks, appreciation and gratitude go to many people, way too many to list here. In addition to everyone I previously acknowledged in the first, second and third editions, I wish to express deep appreciation for my beloved wife Dea Shandera-Hunter, who not only provided daily love, inspiration and support, but also generously shared her heart and soul by reading the manuscript numerous times, patiently sharing ideas and suggestions for making it more readable. Your love and support was and is priceless.

I want to thank my friend and colleague David Christel for his valuable feedback, and for his outstanding expertise with editing, page layout, formatting, and his eagle eye attention to detail.

I also give special thanks to all of my brothers and sisters worldwide who came before me, for we truly stand on the shoulders of the giants who have come before us.

Finally, I would like to call out and thank the following beautiful people who are the first International Ambassadors of Peace for The Rainbow Bridge: Dea Shandera-Hunter, Carmel Maguire, and Marty Lewis. Thank you so much for your tireless efforts to help spread universal principles, peace and harmony in the world, each and every day.

About the Author

With professional certifications in project management, knowledge management and change management, Brent Hunter is the author of four books, an IT professional, producer, former psychotherapist and National Certified Counselor. Hunter is also a social media pioneer as the founder of the first Internet-based global community called "The Park," with more than 700,000 members in 190 countries worldwide. Through the amazing Park Odyssey, which he is now chronicling in a separate book, he learned some of what it means to be a human.

Brent is part Muslim and part Jewish, and was brought up as a Christian. He currently studies and lives by an integrated set of life principles including Bahai'i, Buddhist, Christian, Confucian, Earth-based, Hindu, Islamic, Jewish, Native American/Indigenous, Sikh, and Taoist traditions. Brent believes that all paths are divine and must be equally respected in order for the world to become a significantly better place for all of our brothers and sisters worldwide.

Brent received a B.S. in Math and Computer Science from Clarkson University, an M.S. in Counseling and Human Relations from Villanova University, and the equivalent of an M.S. in Information Systems after he graduated from the General Electric Company's fast-track Information Systems Management Program.

The Rainbow Bridge

Brent is an Eagle Scout, a graduate of the U.S. Army Airborne School, and is involved with a number of global civic organizations, including a past position in the United Nations Association of the U.S. as the Vice President of Communications in the Northern California Division. He is also the author of *The Pieces of Our Puzzle: A Multi-Faceted Approach to Personal Health and Well Being*, *Nuggets of Wisdom: Quotes to Ponder and Inspire*, *More Nuggets of Wisdom: Quotes to Ponder and Inspire*, and the upcoming *The Park Odyssey*.

After being born in Brooklyn, NY and living in Upstate New York, Philadelphia, Chicago and San Francisco, Brent currently lives, plays, and works in Los Angeles. Orion, whose picture was on the back cover of the 2nd edition, peacefully passed over The Rainbow Bridge on April 23rd, 2009.

Contact Information

To order additional books or to contact the author:

Spirit Rising Productions
2261 Market Street, #637
San Francisco, CA 94114

Web: www.TheRainbowBridge.org
Email: Support@TheRainbowBridge.org

If you are aware of any Rainbow Bridge interpretations, physical Rainbow Bridges, Rainbow Bridge stores, etc. that aren't included in this edition, please let us know so that they may be included in a future edition.

Copies of the paperback edition are $12.95 plus $2.50 shipping and handling per book. Copies of the deluxe hardcover edition and the spiral-bound edition are $24.95 plus $4.00 shipping and handling per book.

PART SEVEN

Inspiring Quotations
and Messages

The Rainbow Bridge

A Dream of Peace

"And God says, I have a dream. I have a dream that all of my children will discover that they belong in one family — my family, the human family — a family in which there are no outsiders. All, all belong, all are held in the embrace of this one whose love will never let us go, this one who says that each one of us is of incredible worth, that each one of us has their name written on the palms of God's hands. And God says, there are no outsiders — black, white, red, yellow, short, tall, young, old, rich, poor, gay, lesbian, straight — everyone. All belong. And God says, I have only you to help me realize my dream. Help me."

— Archbishop Desmond Tutu

The Rainbow People

"There is truth in the prophecies of the Rainbow and the Rainbow people. People from all of the Americas will unite with people from all the other nations, and they will realize that we are all Family, brothers and sisters. This is not my personal vision, but the cosmic vision presented by all the elders, a vision that we all share."

— Don Alejandro Cirilo Perez, President of the Maya
Elders Council in Guatemala

Brilliance

"Our biggest fear is not that we are inadequate.
Our deepest fear is that we are powerful beyond measure.
It is our light, not our darkness, that most frightens us.
We ask ourselves, who am I to be brilliant, or gorgeous or talented or
fabulous? Actually, who are you NOT to be?
You are a child of God.
Playing small doesn't serve the world.
There's nothing enlightened about shrinking so that
other people won't feel insecure around you.
We were born to make manifest the
glory of God that is within us.
It's not just in some of us; it's in every one of us.
And as we let our own light shine, we unconsciously
give other people permission to do the same.
As we are liberated from our own fear, our presence automatically
liberates others."

— From *A Return to Love*,
Marianne Williamson

Your Journey Has Just Begun

"Perfection is being right.
Excellence is willing to be wrong.

Perfection is fear.
Excellence is taking a risk.

Perfection is anger and frustration.
Excellence is powerful.

Perfection is control.
Excellence is spontaneous.

Perfection is judgment.
Excellence is accepting.

Perfection is taking.
Excellence is giving.

Perfection is doubt.
Excellence is confidence.

Perfection is pressure.
Excellence is natural.

Perfection is the destination.

The Rainbow Bridge

Excellence is the journey."

— From *You're The Greatest*,
Francis Xavier Maguire

Conflict and Harmony

"The purpose of conflict is to restore harmony."

Let There Be Peace

"Let there be peace and love
between all beings of the universe.

Let there be peace.

Let there be peace.

Om Shanti, Shanti, Shanti."

— Sri H. W. L. Poonja (Poonjaji or Papaji)

The Wikipedia definition of Shanti is:
Shanti, Santhi or Shanthi means peace,
rest, calmness, tranquility, or bliss.

Child of the Universe

"I am a child of the universe —

With the glitter of my life, I travel through black,
velvet space, and the gates of time —

I am a star, awoken from its sleep, by the
longing cries of mankind's dreams —

Dreams of harmony, love, and a child of the universe..."

— From *A Child of the Universe*
Ralph-Armand Beck (DJ Taucher)

Salutation of the Dawn

"…For yesterday is but a dream and tomorrow is only a vision, but today well-lived makes every yesterday a dream of happiness and every tomorrow a vision of hope….

Look well, therefore to this day!

Such is the salutation of the dawn."

— Kalidasa

Discovery

"All truths are easy to understand once they are discovered; the point is to discover them."

— Galileo

Knowing

"Some things can be known, but not understood,
but everything that can be understood can be known."

We Are Spiritual Beings

"We are not physical being having a spiritual experience;
we are spiritual beings having a human experience."

— Teilhard de Chardin

Contemplation and Vision

"A rock pile ceases to be a rock pile the moment a single man contemplates it, bearing within him the image of a cathedral."

— Antoine de Saint-Exupery

The Prophecy of the Eagle and the Condor

"There is a long-told legend and prophecy that says that in the beginning all the people were united as one, but that many years ago they divided into two groups, each group following a different path. One group, known as the Eagle, were highly scientific and intellectual. The other group, the Condors, were highly attuned to nature and the intuitive realm. These two groups continued along their own paths becoming further evolved in their own ways. It was prophesized that both groups would eventually come to a point where their very existence was threatened.

Thus, the Eagle people — those of the intellect and the mind — will have reached a point in their development of their scientific knowledge and technology, and their ability to build and construct so well that it would bring tremendous material wealth but at the same time they would be so spiritually impoverished that their very existence would be at risk.

At the same time the people of the Condor — people of the heart, the spirit, who are deeply connected to the natural world — would become highly developed in their intuitive skills, and in their understanding of the spiritual realm. At the same time they would be hungry and impoverished for knowledge that would enable them to be successful in the material world.

The Rainbow Bridge

The prophecy continues by saying that now is the time for the Eagle people and the Condor people to reunite, to remember that they are actually one people with a common origin. It is time for the eagle and the condor to fly together in the spirit of partnership and collaboration. Neither the eagles nor the condors will survive without this collaboration, and from this new partnership will emerge a new consciousness that will result in a sustainable future for all."

— From *The Soul of Money*,
Lynne Twist

Persistence

"Nothing in the world can take the place of persistence.

Talent will not; nothing is more common than unsuccessful men with talent.

Genius will not; unrewarded genius is almost a proverb.

Education will not; the world is full of educated derelicts.

Persistence and determination alone are omnipotent."

— U.S. President Calvin Coolidge

Perseverance

He failed in business in 1831.
He was defeated for State Legislator in 1832.
He tried another business in 1833. It failed.
His fiancée died in 1835.
He had a nervous breakdown in 1836.

In 1838, he ran for Congress and was defeated.
He tried again in 1839 and was
defeated again.
He tried running for the Senate and lost.
The next year, he ran for Vice President
and lost.
In 1859, he ran for the Senate again and was defeated.
In 1860, the man who signed his name

Abraham Lincoln

was elected
President of the United States

The Serenity Prayer

"God, give us grace to accept with serenity
the things that cannot be changed,
courage to change the things which should be changed,
and the wisdom to distinguish the one from the other."

— Dr. Reinhold Niebuhr/Friedrich Oetinger

About Defects

"No one should abandon duties because he sees defects in them. Every action, every activity, is surrounded by defects as a fire is surrounded by smoke."

— Krishna

Taking Action

"It is not enough to stare up the steps,
we must step up the stairs."

— Vaclav Havel

Whose Job Is It?

"There was a story about four people named Everybody,
Somebody, Anybody and Nobody.

There was an important job to be done and
Everybody was asked to do it.

Everybody was sure Somebody would do it.
Anybody could have done it, but Nobody did it.

Somebody got angry about that, because it was Everybody's job.
Everybody thought Anybody could do it but Nobody realized that
Everybody wouldn't do it.

It ended up that Everybody blamed Somebody when Nobody did
what Anybody could have done."

— Anonymous

All Truths Pass Through Three Stages

"1st: It is ridiculed

2nd: It is violently opposed

3rd: It is accepted as self-evident"

— Schopenhauer

The Rainbow Bridge

The Invitation

"It doesn't interest me what you do for a living.

I want to know what you ache for, and if you dare to
dream of meeting your heart's longing.

It doesn't interest me how old you are.

I want to know if you will risk looking like a fool for love,
for your dream, for the adventure of being alive.

It doesn't interest me what planets are squaring your moon.

I want to know if you have touched the center of your own sorrow,
if you have been opened by life's betrayals, or have become shriveled
and closed from fear of further pain.

I want to know if you can sit with pain, mine or your own,
without moving to hide it or fade it or fix it.

I want to know if you can be with joy, mine or your own; if you can
dance with wildness and let the ecstasy fill you to the tips of your
fingers and toes without cautioning us to be careful, to be realistic,
to remember the limitations of being human.

It doesn't interest me if the story you're telling me is true.

The Rainbow Bridge

I want to know if you can disappoint another to be true to yourself.

If you can bear the accusation of betrayal
and not betray your own soul.

If you can be faithless and therefore trustworthy.

I want to know if you can see beauty, even when it's not pretty,
every day, and if you can source your life from its presence.

I want to know if you can live with failure, yours and mine, and still
stand on the edge of the lake and shout to the sliver of the full moon,
"Yes!"

It doesn't interest me to know where you live
or how much money you have.

I want to know if you can get up, after the night of grief and despair,
weary and bruised to the bone,
and do what needs to be done to feed the children.

It doesn't interest me who you know or how you came to be here.

I want to know if you will stand in the center of the fire
with me and not shrink back.

It doesn't interest me where or what or with whom you have studied.

The Rainbow Bridge

I want to know what sustains you, from the inside,
when all else falls away.

I want to know if you can be alone with yourself and if you truly like
the company you keep in the empty moments."

— From *The Invitation*
Oriah Mountain Dreamer

One Earth, One People

The Original Plan of Creator, Life-Giver:

That we are One People, on One Earth;

That all life is sacred;

That the Earth is sacred;

That we must cherish and protect our Mother Earth,
Father Sky above and Sacred Oceans below;

That the Four Races of Mankind will Live in Harmony with all
Living Things, so that as many as Seven Generations to follow each
Generation (Our Future Generations) will Live.

The Seven Eagle Feathers represent these Future Generations and
our Sacred Ceremonies.

These sacred Feathers carry our prayers to God; Whom we call
Grandfather, Wakan-Tanka, Tunkashila:

That All Our Relations May Live.

The Rainbow Bridge

It is One Prayer:

PEACE

— Laynee Bluebird

Deep Wisdom

"Those who know, do not speak;
those who speak, do not know."

— Tao Te Ching

The Best Way to Predict the Future

"The best way to predict the future
is to create it."

— Dr. Peter Drucker

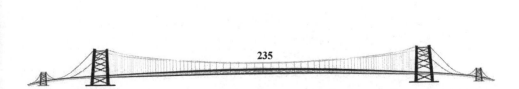

The Rainbow Bridge

We Are One

"At the level of consciousness,
humanity is One."

— Yogiraj Satgurunath Siddhanath

Bliss

"Follow your bliss."

— Joseph Campbell

The Sun Is Always Shining

"The sunshine is always shining
above the clouds."

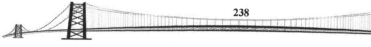

Making Peace with Your Enemies

"If you want to make peace with your enemy,
you have to work with your enemy.
Then he becomes your partner."

— Nelson Mandela

Hope

"Hope is like a road in the country.
There was never a road, but when many people walk on it,
the road comes into existence."

— Lin Yutang

Waking Up

"Lose your head and come to your senses."

— Fritz Perls

Progress

"In order for progress to occur,
two generations must agree."

— From the movie *Wag the Dog*

Why Are We Here?

"Why are we here?

To love, bless, inspire and uplift one another."

Deep Vitality

"Seek out that particular mental attribute which makes you feel most deeply and vitally alive, along with which comes the inner voice which says, 'This is the real me,' and when you have found that attitude, follow it."

— Dr. William James

You Are Here to Change the World

"Inside of you is a magnificence that's waiting to reveal itself, that's waiting to make a difference. There's an evolutionary impulse in every cell of your being. Wanting to come forth, wanting to be shared, wanting to shift, wanting to make a difference, wanting to be a contribution.....

There is a power within you that is here to shift the face of this planet, and the way we live with one another...forever.

The time to allow that magnificent, infinite power to shine forth, to shine through you, is *now*. The power to change you and this planet is within you. Slow down and look within. *You are needed, now. You are here to change the world.*"

— Panache Desai

The Future Is Knocking On Our Door

"The future is knocking at our door right now. Make no mistake, the next generation *will* ask us one of two questions. Either they will ask: 'What were you thinking; why didn't you act?'

Or they will ask instead: 'How did you find the moral courage to rise and successfully resolve a crisis that so many said was impossible to solve?'

We have everything we need to get started, save perhaps political will, but political will is a renewable resource.

So let us renew it, and say together: 'We have a purpose. We are many. For this purpose we will rise, and we will act.'"

— U.S. Vice President Al Gore,
2007 Nobel Acceptance Speech

The Rainbow Bridge

Index

The Rainbow Bridge

The Rainbow Bridge

The Rainbow Bridge

The Rainbow Bridge

The Rainbow Bridge

The Rainbow Bridge

The Rainbow Bridge

The Rainbow Bridge

The Rainbow Bridge

The Rainbow Bridge

Conscious Intentions

May you, all your relations and all beings everywhere be
showered with love, compassion, wisdom, happiness,
joy, peace, bliss, ecstasy, appreciation, dedication,
devotion, commitment, abundance, prosperity,
and pleasure…now and in all times.

May peace, abundance, and joy return to Earth.

From My Heart

All My Relations

Epilogue

Was this book too simple? Did it feel like it was just for beginners? If so, welcome to the crowd. And don't forget that *life is not always as it appears.*

It is not by chance that you are reading this book. Now that you have it in your hands, *keep it and read it again from time to time,* and don't be surprised if you start to see it in a different way each time you read it. Flip it open to a random page to see what message synchronistically appears…and remember that it is not accidental.

Most of all, don't be surprised if you start to see yourself as a beautiful character in a dream waking up to the concept that *you are much more than the character you play in this dream of life….*

You are now on the
next page of your life and
you are already there...

Made in the USA
San Bernardino, CA
20 February 2018